MW01492888

Dining On A Dime Cookbook
Gluten Free Dairy Free Edition

1st Printing: November 2020
2nd Printing: October 2021

ISBN: 978-1-7341350-3-9

Copyright 2020 Kellam Media And Publishing, Inc. dba Living On A Dime

All rights reserved. No part of this book may be reproduced in any form, except brief excerpts for the purpose of review, without written permission of the publisher.

Designed, Produced and Published by:
Kellam Media and Publishing, Inc.
P.O. Box 193
Mead, CO 80542
editor@livingonadime.com

Printed in Korea

The author and publisher specifically disclaim any liability, loss or risk, personal or otherwise which is incurred as a consequence, directly or indirectly, of the use and application of any of the contents of this book.

Anecdotes are author unknown unless specified.

Graphics by David Kellam, the best middle child ever. Thanks, Dave!

About The Authors

Tawra Kellam and Jill Cooper are a mother-daughter team who share their recipes and tips for saving money at LivingOnADime.com.

As a single mother of two, Jill started her own business without any capital and paid off $35,000 of debt in 5 years on $1,000 a month income.

She then raised two teenagers alone on $500 a month income after becoming disabled with Chronic Fatigue Syndrome.

In five years, Tawra and her husband, Mike, paid off $20,000 of personal debt at a time when their average income was $22,000 per year.

Tawra, inspired by her mom's ways to stretch money beyond what anyone would think possible, decided to write the first edition of the Dining On A Dime Cookbook in 1997 under the title Not Just Beans.

Dining On A Dime Cookbook has been in continuous publication since its first edition in 1999, with over 500,000 books sold. Tawra and Jill are known worldwide for their easy recipes and for getting dinner on the table without a lot of hassle.

Using the recipes and tips in this book, hundreds of thousands of people have saved thousands of dollars each on their grocery bills and are living less stressful lives, thanks to Tawra and Jill's tips.

The recipes cards in this book are the original recipe cards from 5 generations of Tawra's family. The recipes feature Tawra's mom, 5 grandmothers and her daughter. It was a true family endeavor spanning 70 years!

Table Of Contents

Basics Of
GFDF Cooking

Eat Better And Spend Less While Eating Gluten Free Dairy Free

There are a lot of tasty gluten free dairy free recipes and it's actually quite easy to eat GF and DF. It is hard to go from wonderful breads and desserts that you love to feeling like you "can't eat anything".

The truth is you can eat a LOT of things that still taste great. When it comes to yeast breads, they may not be "exactly" the same but they can still be very tasty. There are many GF DF cookies and desserts you would never know were gluten free and dairy free.

I have been GF DF for 10 years and I used my Dining On A Dime Cookbook to cook 90% of my recipes. My assistant Heidi suggested that I should adapt Dining On A Dime to be GF DF, so other people could use it as I have done and that is what I've done with this book. Even though a lot of these recipes are "naturally" GF DF, this book is written to give you ideas about all the great things you can eat on a GF DF diet.

I have personally tested all the recipes. I made sure that they were either undetectable as GF DF or VERY close to the "real" thing. I tested them on my "normal" family and friends and they were totally shocked how great these recipes tasted.

Don't be intimidated by GF DF cooking and baking. Start with easy things like cookies and brownies and then move into "harder" things like breads. (They really aren't that hard.)

Just keep practicing and you will get it down.

Basics Of
Gluten Free Dairy Free Cooking

Important!!!

READ THE DIRECTIONS. I repeat, **READ THE DIRECTIONS!!**
90% of the time when I had a GF DF recipe fail, it was because I
didn't read **AND FOLLOW** the directions **EXACTLY** as the recipe was
written. **THIS IS VERY IMPORTANT!**

I don't know how many times I have read bad reviews on recipes or
gotten emails from people saying a recipe "was just awful" only to find
that they didn't follow the directions or make the recipe the way it was
written. Make the recipe **EXACTLY** as it's written first before making
substitutions or changing the recipe.

Make sure that you **don't** confuse **gluten free baking mix** with
gluten free all purpose flour. They are **NOT** the same. GF Baking
Mix has additional baking powder already included in the mix so that
will affect how your recipe turns out.

Don't become overwhelmed. Read the book, try one or two recipes
and tips and keep building from there. It's not hard but it is a new way
of baking.

Don't get discouraged if a recipe fails. All of these recipes have
been tested (The bread was tested 25 times!) and they **DO** work.
Some things, like learning to bake gluten free and dairy free, take time
and practice, but in the end you can save money and you will learn
new skills.

Most foods have satisfaction guarantees on the products. If you
don't like a product like a gluten free flour or new dairy free milk,
return it to the store or call the toll free number on the back of the box.
A lot of companies will either give you your money back or send you a
coupon for another product.

Gluten Free Flours

Gluten free all purpose flour comes in many varieties. The most common is a rice flour base. Try several and see which you prefer. They are not all the same.

YOU MUST spoon the flour into your measuring cup and then level. **DO NOT, I REPEAT DO NOT** scoop it out of the bag. You will get too much flour and then your baking will be heavy instead of light and fluffy.

Here are the gluten free all purpose flours that I prefer, in order of my preference (in 2020):

- Great Value Gluten Free All Purpose Flour from Walmart (cheapest brand I found)

- Pamela's Gluten Free Artisan All Purpose Flour

- King Arthur Gluten Free All Purpose Flour

Gluten Free Baking Mix

The difference between gluten free all purpose flour and gluten free baking mix is that baking mix already includes additional baking powder and sometimes salt and shortening.

My favorite gluten free baking mixes:

- Great Value Gluten Free Baking Mix from Walmart (cheapest brand I found)

- Pamela's Baking Mix

- King Arthur Baking Mix

Again, make sure that you **don't** get **gluten free baking mix** and **gluten free all purpose flour** mixed up. They are **NOT** the same. GF Baking Mix has additional baking powder in the mix so that will affect how your recipe turns out.

I know I'm repeating myself but this is the **NUMBER ONE** mistake that people make when their gluten free baking doesn't turn out.

Xanthan Gum

Xanthan gum is a popular food additive that's commonly added to foods as a thickener or stabilizer. It makes a great thickening, suspending and stabilizing agent for many products.

Some gluten free all purpose flour comes with xanthan gum (or guar gum) and some comes without it. If you use a gluten free flour **WITHOUT** xanthan gum, then you will need to add it to help the recipe stay together and be fluffier.

Dairy Free Butter Options

There are many good dairy free butter options out there. Some are more expensive made with olive and avocado oils and some are cheaper and mostly use soy oils. Which dairy free butter you use is really just a matter of preference. I've tested almost every one to date and they all worked just fine.

You can use shortening in place of butter or margarine for most baking. Dairy free butter may be used, but it is more expensive.

I prefer butter flavored shortening for most baking. If you can't find it in your store, you can use regular shortening and add 1 tsp. butter flavoring.

If you want to try other oils like coconut oil for baking, you will just have to try each recipe and see how it works. I only tested with shortening and dairy free butters.

Vinegar

You will notice a lot of the baking recipes call for vinegar or apple cider vinegar. **DO NOT** leave it out. It helps the dough rise.

Cooking Spray

Most cooking sprays (Pam) are gluten free and dairy free, but be careful to check the ingredients because some do contain flour.

Dairy Free Milk

If I have a type of milk listed in parentheses in a recipe, that is the milk I prefer and used for testing, but others can be used.

Some options for dairy free milk (in order of my preference) are:

- rice milk
- soy milk
- almond milk
- coconut milk
- flax milk
- cashew milk
- hemp milk
- oat milk

Each dairy free milk works differently in different recipes. Coconut milk has a higher fat content and is better for recipes like puddings. Rice, soy and flax milk have a more neutral taste and work better for recipes like ranch dressing. You may need to experiment to see which ones you like the best.

Different dairy free milks also have different tastes. You may not want to use coconut milk in ranch dressing but it would be great in chocolate pudding. So just ask yourself, "Do I want this to taste like coconut?" or cashews or whatever when you decide which dairy free milk to use.

Dairy Free Cheese

Dairy free cheese can be hit or miss. These are the ones that I use and prefer:

- Daiya
- Violife
- Follow your heart
- Lisanatti

General Gluten Free Dairy Free Baking Rules

Important!!

Mix Well!
When baking breads and cookies with gluten free flour, you want to make sure that you **THOROUGHLY** mix the batter. For gluten free bread, that will mean 3-5 minutes mixing with the mixer.

Room Temperature Ingredients
Make sure all your ingredients are at room temperature. This is especially important for gluten free yeast bread baking.

Longer Baking Time
A lot of gluten free baking will take a few minutes longer to bake. I have adjusted the time in this cookbook so recipe times are correct for gluten free, but if you are trying to turn "regular" recipes into gluten free, you may need to bake 5-15 minutes longer. Just test your recipes with the longest cooking time suggested and then add as needed.

DON'T Open The Door!
Do NOT open the door when making gluten free yeast breads and cakes until the minimum bake time has been reached. Slamming the door can cause breads and cakes to fall.

Use A Meat Thermometer
To double check that yeast bread or rolls are finished baking, use an instant read meat thermometer to check the internal temperature. A perfectly baked yeast loaf will reach an internal temperature of 202-205 degrees or 200 degrees at high altitude.

Let Cool!
Make sure you let cookies and cakes cool completely before removing from the pan.

Don't Let It Cool In The Pan!
Yeast loaf breads should not be completely cooled in the pan. The steam can build up and cause soggy bread. Let cool 10 minutes and then remove from the pan to cool the rest of the way.

Gluten Free Dairy Free
High Altitude Baking Rules

Baking Powder

Above 6,000 feet: reduce by ¼ teaspoon for each teaspoon

Above 8,000 feet: reduce by ½ teaspoon for each teaspoon

Rise Time In Yeast Breads

Reduce the rise time of yeast breads. DO NOT let the dough rise higher than the side of the pan. Check frequently to ensure bread is not rising more than double its size before baking. If it does, it will overflow the pan. If that happens, put a cookie sheet underneath to catch the overflow and bake anyway. It won't be pretty but it might still be edible.

Muffins

Do not fill muffins or cake pans more than ½ full.

Salt

Do not omit salt in yeast bread recipes because salt will help to contain the rise.

Increase Baking Temperature

Try increasing the baking temperature by 25° to help set the cell structure faster so that it is better supported after cooling.

Eggs

•   Use extra large eggs instead of large eggs. (Eggs contain protein, which helps to provide structure.)

•   Do not over-beat eggs. This will enhance the rising of batters, which is not advised at high altitudes.

Crumbly And Dry

If the recipe turns out drier and more crumbly than it ought to be:

- **6,000 feet:** Increase liquid by 2 tablespoons
- **7,000 feet:** Increase liquid by 3-5 tablespoons
- **OR** decrease gluten free flour by 1 tablespoon per cup of flour.
- Add 1-2 Tablespoons of honey to help hold moisture.
- Try substituting shortening for butter – it holds more liquid.

Undercooked

If your baked goods aren't fully cooked (wet inside or dense):

- Some cakes and breads, which bake under an hour at sea level, can take as long as 1 hour and 30 minutes to bake at high altitude. Reduce the oven temperature to 325° and bake longer, checking frequently with a toothpick or internal thermometer to make sure it is fully cooked before removing to cool.

If Cookies Flatten

- Reduce the shortening by 1-2 tablespoons.
- Substitute shortening for butter.
- Add ⅛ cup more gluten free all purpose flour per each cup of flour in the recipe.
- Reduce the amount of additions like chocolate chips.
- Add a tablespoon or so of powdered milk or non-dairy powdered milk (not reconstituted).

If Your Pie Crusts Or Pastries Are Dry Or Tough

- Reduce gluten free all purpose flour or use less flour to dust with and handle the crust as little as possible.
- Ensure the fats (butter, oil, shortening) and liquids are very cold when mixing.
- Increase liquid by up to 25%.

Don't Make GF DF Eating Complicated.

When starting out with gluten free and dairy free eating and cooking, don't make it so complicated. Start making easy things, like chicken and rice, tacos with corn tortillas and roast with potatoes and vegetables.

Instead of:

Flour tortillas - Use corn tortillas.

Dinner rolls - Use rice.

Biscuits - Use roasted potatoes.

Frosted flakes - Use Rice Chex.

Cheese - Either leave it off or get dairy free cheese.

Bread - Just buy gluten free bread for the person or people who need it. It is expensive, but when you consider 1 loaf of GF bread lasts me two weeks, that's not bad.

Bread crumbs - Use oatmeal or cornmeal when mixed into recipes like meatloaf. Use cornmeal for coating things like fish.

Dips and salad dressings - Use salsa, guacamole, oil and vinegar, Italian dressing, Dorothy Lynch, Thousand Island, poppyseed, hummus, mayonnaise (with or without seasonings) and homemade dressing made with rice milk and mayonnaise.

Chocolate chips - There are some really good dairy free chocolate chips available now.

Sweetened condensed milk - Use sweetened condensed coconut milk.

Meal Ideas

Keep a master list of menus. For one month, keep track of what you have for every dinner. Then, you will have a list to go by so you don't have to spend a lot of time planning future meals.

I don't plan meals one or two weeks in advance. I prefer to do it only a couple of days in advance. If I planned too far ahead, I wouldn't be able to take advantage of deals that I find. (I just found 14 avocados for .99 on the clearance shelf. I didn't plan for this but it was a great treat!) I hope these menu suggestions help you get started. Enjoy!

Breakfasts

Fried eggs
Bacon
Hash browns
GF Toast
Juice

Apple pancakes
    add 1 chopped apple to
    GF pancake batter
Sausage patties or bacon
Hash browns
Grapefruit half

Sliced ham
Scrambled eggs
Fried potatoes
Orange juice

Waffles
Eggs, scrambled or fried
Bacon or sausage
Fresh fruit, sliced

Crepes
Bacon
Cantaloupe Slices

Poached Eggs on
GF toast buttered with DF butter
Fresh strawberries and bananas

GF English muffins
    filled with scrambled egg,
    sliced ham and DF cheese
Apple slices

Omelets
Fried potatoes
GF muffins
Grapes

Oatmeal with
    Butter, brown sugar, raisins
    or dried apples

Millet with
    Butter, sugar, raisins
    or dried apples

Scrambled eggs
GF toast
Bacon
Juice

Poultry

Maple glazed chicken
Cucumber salad
Rice
Glazed carrots

Mexican chicken
Spanish rice
Steamed broccoli
Sliced tomatoes

Chicken and GF dumplings
Tossed salad
Green beans

Roast chicken
Rice
Steamed broccoli
Orange slices

Chicken tacos
Spanish rice

Chicken soup
GF crackers
Relish dish
    carrots, celery, cauliflower,
    broccoli
Dip

Honey baked chicken
Baked squash
Sliced tomatoes

Chicken pot pie
Cauliflower and broccoli with dip
Baked apples
Fruit gelatin

Barbecue chicken
Potato salad
Corn on the cob
Sliced cucumbers
Fresh or frozen sliced peaches

Baked chicken
Brown rice
Sliced cucumbers and tomatoes

Chicken sandwich on
    GF toasted bread with
    lettuce and tomato
Cantaloupe slices

Grilled chicken breasts
Rice
Fruit salad

Chicken and GF noodles
Fresh fruit

Chicken and rice soup
Sliced cucumbers, carrots
    and broccoli with DF ranch
    dressing

Chicken fajitas
Chips and salsa

Barbecue chicken pizza
Sliced fruit

Chicken salad sandwiches
Pickles
Sliced cucumbers, carrots
    and broccoli with DF ranch
    dressing

Roast Turkey
Cucumber salad
Sweet potato casserole

Beef

Sloppy Joes on GF buns
GF French fries
Sliced oranges

Meatloaf
Tossed salad
Mashed potatoes
Red applesauce
    sprinkle with red gelatin
    straight from the box

Meatloaf
Potato patties
Carrot and celery sticks

Chicken fried steak
GFDF gravy
Mashed potatoes
Steamed mixed vegetables
Sliced tomatoes

Hamburgers
    with lettuce, DF cheese &
    tomatoes
Cole slaw
GF French fries
Baked beans

GF Spaghetti with
Meatballs
Tossed salad

Barbecue meatballs
Baked potatoes
Green beans

Hamburger casserole
Sliced tomatoes or
Corn on the cob

Tacos
Refried beans
Tortilla chips with honey

Fajitas in corn tortillas
Mexican corn
Tortilla chips with salsa

Pepper steak over
Rice
Broccoli

Swiss steak
Fresh spinach salad
Baked potatoes

Hot roast beef sandwich
Garden salad
Mashed potatoes
Whole kernel corn

Stew
Muffins

Beef and noodles
Steamed broccoli
Pineapple orange gelatin

Slow cooked roast
Brown gravy
Tossed salad and dressing
Onions, carrots, potatoes
    cooked with roast

Barbecued beef
Potato salad
Baked beans
Sliced cucumber
Watermelon

Beef stroganoff
Garden salad

Barbecue ribs in crockpot
Cole slaw
GF cornbread

Pork

Peachy pork chops
Carrot and celery sticks
Baked potato

Polish sausage
Brussels sprouts
Oven fried potatoes

Sausage patties
GF cornbread
Fried potatoes
Sliced bananas and strawberries

Ham and beans
Carrot salad
GF cornbread

Maple glazed ham
Au gratin potatoes
Steamed broccoli
Fruit salad

Ham slices, fried
Sweet potatoes
Applesauce
    with cinnamon and sugar

Ham and potatoes
Minty peas and onions

Sliced ham
Tossed salad and dressing
Baked potatoes

Meatless

Tomato soup
GFDF Grilled cheese sandwich
Celery sticks and dip

Potato soup
Baked apples

Broccoli soup
Sliced fruit
GF crackers

Vegetable soup
GF crackers and DF cheese

Chili
GF crackers

Bean soup
GF crackers

Chef salad

GF spaghetti
Tossed salad

Jumbo baked potato
    Toppings: broccoli, bacon,
    DF cheese, tomatoes,
    DF sour cream, chili,
    cubed ham

Lunch Ideas

GF Granola

GFDF Quesadillas

Omelets

GF Spaghetti

GF cereal/oatmeal with fruit

GFDF grilled cheese sandwich

GFDF tuna, egg or chicken salad sandwich

Tuna salad and GF crackers

Soup and GF crackers

Scrambled egg with DF cheese

GF turkey sandwiches

GFDF macaroni and cheese

Hot dogs (not for children 3 and under)

GFDF Pizza cut into bite-size pieces

Salad

Refried beans: Spread on GF toast and sprinkle with DF cheese. Broil until cheese bubbles.

GF toast with some spaghetti sauce & DF cheese melted on top

Rice with a vegetable, mixed with teriyaki sauce

GFDF Hot ham and cheese sandwich: Toast GF bread. Melt DF cheese and warm the ham on the bread in the microwave.

Ants on a log: Serve celery with peanut butter inside and raisins on the peanut butter.

Canned baked beans. Hot dog slices or a spoon of plain DF yogurt may be added.

GF noodles with GFDF cream-of-something soup (mushroom or broccoli)

- **To keep drinks cold in lunch boxes, pour a small amount of the drink in the bottom of the container (not glass) and then set the cap loosely on top. Put it in the freezer overnight. The next day, fill with the rest of the drink. The ice should slowly melt all day long, keeping the beverage cool.**

- **Save the ketchup and mustard packets and napkins you don't use from fast food restaurants. Use them in lunch boxes.**

Snack Ideas

Fresh fruit

Apples, cut into quarters

Apples, quartered with 1 tsp.
    peanut butter on each

Dried fruit

Oranges, peeled and quartered

Bananas

Bananas, sliced in half and
    spread with peanut butter

Frozen grapes (p.300)

Veggies with DF ranch dressing
    (p.166)

Celery sticks, spread with peanut
    butter

Cherry tomatoes

Strawberry leather (p.306)

DF puddings (p.307)

GF granola bars (p.297)

GF cinnamon sugar toast with tea

DF cocoa

DF creamy orange shake (p.40)

GF pretzels

Pork rinds

Potato chips

Tortilla chips and salsa

Fruit smoothies (p.42-43)

Hard boiled eggs

Popcorn balls

Popcorn

GFDF muffins (p.56-60)

Banana bread (p.96)

Zucchini cake (p.234)

Pumpkin bread (p.97)

GF crackers and DF cheese

GF crackers spread with peanut
    butter and jelly or jam

GF cookies (p.271-283)

Beef jerky (p.175)

GF bread or toast spread with
    jelly, jam, peanut butter,
    spiced honey (p.343),
    or DF honey butter (p.342)

GF trail mix

Olives

Nuts

Pickles

GF crackers and hummus

Rice cakes with peanut butter or
    DF cheese

GF Chex Mix

Meal Plan

Shopping List

Monday
_____
_____
_____

Tuesday
_____
_____
_____

Wednesday
_____
_____
_____

Thursday
_____
_____
_____

Friday
_____
_____
_____

Saturday
_____
_____
_____

Sunday
_____
_____
_____

Notes
_____
_____
_____
_____
_____

How To Save On Herbs

- **Buy spices in bulk** from spice shops or from mail order companies. Sometimes they have minimum orders. If so, split the order with your friends and family.

- **Grow your own herbs.** One herb plant is enough to supply you for a year with dried herbs. Place one herb plant in a 6 inch pot or two or three herb plants in a 15 inch pot. Fill to two inches from the top with dirt. Place in a sunny window or in a sunny spot in the yard. Water when the soil becomes dry, as needed. Do not over water and do not fertilize herbs.

- **To use fresh herbs:** Harvest one or two stems from the plant. Strip leaves from stem and cut leaves into small pieces. Discard stems.

- **To dry herbs:** In the fall before the first frost, cut the stems at the base of the plant. Tie the bottom of the stems together with a rubber band. Hang to dry upside down in a cool dark place for several weeks. When dry, strip the leaves from the stems and crush leaves to desired consistency. Store in an airtight container.

- **Chives do not dry well** but you can wash them, let them dry and then cut into small pieces and freeze in a freezer bag. Just use as many as you need.

- **Chop a large quantity of parsley** and pack into freezer bags. Freeze. Take out a tablespoon as needed.

Herb Guide

Beef: thyme, celery, marjoram, coriander, sage, rosemary, oregano, garlic

Chicken: garlic, marjoram, tarragon, oregano, coriander

Fish, fried: mustard, oregano, tarragon, sage

Fish, grilled: thyme, coriander, fennel, rosemary

Pork: marjoram, mustard, oregano, sage, rosemary, thyme, garlic

Roast beef: basil, oregano, thyme, mustard, rosemary, garlic

Turkey: basil, rosemary, cumin, oregano, thyme, sage

Basil: tomatoes, tomato sauces, peas, squash, lamb, fish, eggs, tossed salad, goat cheese, potatoes, pasta

Bay leaf: vegetable and fish soups, tomato sauces, poached fish and meat stews

Dill: fish, goat cheese, potatoes, vegetable salads, pickles, tomatoes

Marjoram: fish, vegetable soups, DF cheese dishes, stew, roast chicken, beef, pork, stuffing

Mint: jellies, fruit juices, candies, frostings, cakes, pies, pork, potatoes, peas, and chocolate

Oregano: tomato sauces, pork, pizza, vegetable, fish, salads, chili

Parsley: meats, vegetables, GFDF soups, eggs, DF cheese

Rosemary: GF poultry stuffing, potatoes, cauliflower, fish

Sage: GF stuffing, pork roast, sausage, poultry, and hamburgers

Savory: eggs, meats, salads, chicken, GFDF soups, and GF stuffing

Tarragon: fish sauces, egg and DF cheese dishes, green salads, pickles, chicken, tomatoes, GFDF sauces for meats, and vegetables

Thyme: GFDF soups, GF stuffing, beef, pork dishes, eggs, DF cheese, fish, bean and vegetable soups

What's In Tawra's Pantry?

An essential element of cooking frugally is keeping a well stocked pantry. The concept of a pantry is more than storage. Your pantry should be a place where you always have a good supply of basic ingredients and a few less expensive convenience foods.

When you have the opportunity to buy something that you use frequently at a great price, buy extra and keep it in the pantry until the next time you can get such a good price. This allows you to opt not to buy an item except when the price is very low, "flexing" your pantry.

Here is a list of items that we keep stocked in our pantry virtually all the time. I plan meals around what I have in the pantry and I buy what is on sale to keep my pantry well stocked.

You may want to copy the pantry list for your grocery shopping list.

Just about the time
you can make ends meet,
someone moves the end.

Pantry/Shopping List

Baking Supplies
___ baking powder
___ baking soda
___ DF chocolate chips
___ cocoa
___ coconut
___ cornstarch
___ eggs
___ food coloring
___ lemon juice
___ salt
___ vinegar
___ yeast

Beverages
___ coffee
___ flavored drink mix
___ orange juice
___ tea

Breads
___ GF graham crackers
___ GF crackers
___ GF bread

Cereals
___ Rice Chex
___ Cheerios
___ Fruity Pebbles
___ cream of rice
___ grits
___ GF oatmeal
___ millet
___ buckwheat

Cheeses
___ DF Cheddar

Cooking Oil
___ cooking spray
___ olive oil
___ shortening
___ vegetable oil

Dairy
___ DF butter
___ DF sour cream
___ coconut sweetened
     condensed milk
___ DF milk
___ coconut coffee creamer,
     powdered

Grains
___ cornmeal
___ popcorn
___ GF flour
___ GF baking mix
___ rice

Fruits
___ apples
___ grapefruits
___ oranges
___ peaches
___ pears
___ pineapple
___ raisins

Meats
___ bacon
___ beef roast
___ chicken
___ ground beef
___ ground turkey
___ ham
___ pork chops
___ round steak

Pasta
___ GF noodles

Vegetables
___ broccoli
___ carrots
___ corn
___ green beans
___ green peppers
___ instant mashed
     potatoes
___ lettuce
___ mushrooms
___ onions
___ potatoes
___ tomatoes

Misc. Canned Goods
___ canned tomatoes
___ dried beans
___ mushrooms, canned
___ peanut butter
___ pork and beans
___ pumpkin
___ spaghetti sauce
___ GFDF soup

Misc.
___ potato chips
___ tortilla chips
___ pork rinds
___ marshmallows
___ sunflower seeds
___ pumpkin seeds
___ canned coconut milk
___ flavored gelatins
___ DF ice cream
___ nuts
___ olives

Sugars
___ brown sugar
___ corn syrup
___ honey
___ powdered sugar
___ white sugar

Condiments
___ barbecue sauce
___ ketchup
___ jam/jelly
___ mayonnaise
___ mustard
___ pickles
___ DF salad dressing
___ salsa

Seasonings/Flavorings
___ bouillon - beef, chicken
___ maple extract
___ peppermint extract
___ vanilla

Spices And Herbs
___ allspice
___ basil
___ chili powder
___ cinnamon
___ cinnamon sticks
___ cloves, ground and
     whole
___ cream of tartar
___ cumin
___ garlic powder/garlic salt
___ ginger
___ marjoram
___ nutmeg
___ onion powder/onion salt
___ oregano
___ pepper
___ rosemary
___ salt
___ thyme
___ GF soy sauce
___ Tabasco sauce
___ Worcestershire sauce

Freezer Guide
How long will food keep?

Beef . . . . 12 months

Cakes, cookies and breads . . . . 3-4 months

Coconut . . . . 12 months

Cooked meats . . . . 3 months

Egg whites, out of shell . . . . 12 months

Egg yolks, out of shell . . . . 3 months
(Add ⅛ tsp. salt or ½ tsp. sugar
    for every 4 egg yolks)

Fruits and juices . . . . 12 months

Ground meats . . . . 3 months

DF ice cream . . . . 4 months

Lamb . . . . 9 months

Liver . . . . 2 months

Nuts . . . . 12 months

Pork . . . . 6 months

Poultry, raw . . . . 6 months

Vegetables . . . . 12 months

Recipes That Freeze Well

Barbecued Beef (p.176)

Barbecued Meatballs (p.174)

Bean Goulash (p.183)

Burritos (p.182)

Fajitas (freeze filling ingredients) (p.181)

Green Chile (without the tortillas) (p.204)

Ham and Beans (p.202)

Hash (p.183)

Meatloaf (p.185)

Mexican Chicken (p.197)

Roast Turkey And Gravy (p.190-191) (Bake turkey, freeze turkey and gravy in meal-size portions.)

Shepherd's Pie (p.186)

Sloppy Joes (p.112)

Tawra's #1 Tip For Dinner In 5 Minutes!

To make cooking quick and easy, I always brown 5-10 pounds of ground beef at a time, then divide into ½ pound portions and store in fold top baggies. I store the baggies in the freezer in a large gallon freezer bag. I do the same when roasting turkey or chicken.

This saves time cooking dinner when the meat is already pre-cooked and I just have to throw it together with the flavorings, warm and serve. This also saves space in the freezer when you find a good deal on meat and need to stock up.

Freezer Tips

- **To vacuum seal your freezer bags:** Zip up your freezer bag almost all the way. Leave a hole and put a straw in it. Suck out all the air, quickly remove the straw and seal the bag the rest of the way.

- **To freeze one serving of leftovers:** Place plastic wrap or foil in a muffin tin. Put the leftovers on the plastic wrap, seal and label. Freeze. Remove from muffin tin and store several in a freezer bag. Keep frozen until you need an instant "TV dinner".

- **Fill milk cartons, water bottles, or soft drink bottles** three quarters full with water and place in the freezer to fill up extra space. This makes the freezer use less energy and makes things stay frozen better. These can also be used in coolers or while camping.

- **If there is a power outage,** do not open the freezer unless absolutely necessary. Should you need food, know what you need to get out of the freezer ahead of time. Quickly get what you need, leaving the door open for just a few seconds and quickly shut the door securely. During a power outage, a full freezer of food will usually stay frozen for three days. In a half full freezer, food will usually stay frozen for a couple days.

- **If you need to remove the package from frozen food** such as hamburger without defrosting: Dip it in warm water for a couple of minutes just until the plastic loosens. Remove from package. Brown the frozen hamburger right away.

- **Freeze gluten free flours** to make them last longer.

- **Store nuts in a bag in the freezer.** Remove directly from the freezer and use as needed.

- **Slow cook a roast,** shred, add barbecue sauce, and divide it into individual containers to have barbecue sandwiches anytime!

- **Cook chicken, pork chops, lasagna or meatloaf and freeze.** When you need a quick meal, simply reheat it. (350° is a reliable oven temperature.) Be sure to consider the amount/thickness of the dish when heating.

- **When meat has reached its limit of freezer time,** defrost and cook it. Then freeze cooked meat for meals.

- **Freeze bananas for breads, cakes and shakes.** Just peel and throw in a freezer bag. Mash after defrosting. Two to three large bananas are enough for one loaf of banana bread. Bananas can also be frozen whole in the peel. To use: Defrost, cut off the end and squeeze banana out. It is already mashed.

- **For foods that will darken (like bananas),** add ⅛ teaspoon lemon juice to keep them from browning in the freezer.

- **To freeze apples:** Peel, quarter and slice a few at a time. Drop immediately into cold salt water. Place in freezer bags. The salt water prevents them from darkening. Use for pies, applesauce and apple butters.

- **When you have several oranges or lemons,** wash them thoroughly. Grate the peel before using and freeze the zest.

- **When onions or green peppers are on sale,** buy a large quantity and chop into pieces. Freeze on a tray and then put into freezer bags. Later, take out what you need and return the rest to the freezer. Use for cooked dishes only!

- **Collect all the odds and ends from the garden** at the end of the season. Wash, dry, and freeze together for vegetable soup.

- **Place all pre-made meals in one part of the freezer.** That way your husband and kids can easily find the meals when you aren't home.

Keep a container in the door of the freezer

1. **Dump 1 or 2 tablespoons of hamburger into the container** every time you brown hamburger. At the end of a week or two you will have a "free" meal.

2. **Add to a container any leftovers** like small pieces of meat, sauces or gravies, soups and vegetables that could be used for a soup or stew. Everything but fruit and bread can go in it, even leftover hot breakfast cereal. This is much easier than fighting about eating leftovers. Thaw and add some spices for a hot stew in the winter.

3. **Keep another container for things that would make a good pot pie.** This is especially good for vegetables that get overripe before you use them.

Notes

Beverages

Beverage Tips

- **Be careful to shop wisely.** Sometimes buying name brand, flavored, or specialty coffees on sale costs less than making your own.

- **Drink water.** One quarter to one third of most American's grocery bill is spent on drinks, drink mixes and sugar for the mixes. Cut down on the amount of coffee, tea, juice, milk and pop that your family drinks. Kids don't need juice, pop or a lot of milk. They can drink water. It is just a matter of teaching them to drink water instead of other things.

- **Use powdered coconut milk creamer** instead of creamer in coffee or tea.

- **Buy regular grind coffee and regrind it** into a powder at home. You need to use much less to achieve the same flavor as regular grind coffee.

- **If you run out of coffee filters,** use a paper towel until you can get to the store to buy more.

- **You don't always have to make a full pot of coffee.** Just make one or two cups at a time.

- **Save extra coffee in a thermos** instead of making a new batch or buy a smaller coffee maker.

- **Use 1 tea bag to make 2 or 3 cups of tea** if you don't like it strong. Keep the tea bag in a cup in the refrigerator.

- **Put 1 tea bag in a thermos or teapot** and fill with water. Then you can have hot tea all day long.

- **Put 1 mint leaf or lemon balm leaf** in each ice cube tray section. Pour water over the top and freeze. Then you will have a decorative ice cube for your iced tea.

- **After making coffee, save the coffee filter** and the coffee grounds in the maker. Add your coffee for the next day on top of the old grounds. This way you can use each filter 2 or 3 times.

- **Buy a reusable coffee filter.** They last for years.

Hot Cocoa

¼   cup plus 1 Tbsp. baking cocoa
½   cup sugar
      dash of salt
4   cups dairy free milk (rice, soy or coconut)
¾   tsp. vanilla

Combine cocoa, sugar and salt in a saucepan. Add milk and vanilla, whisk to combine and then warm. Serves 4.

Hot Cocoa Mix

½   cup baking cocoa*
¾   cup coconut milk powder
1   cup sugar
¼   tsp. salt

Mix the ingredients in a bowl and store in a covered container. May be doubled or tripled as needed.

To prepare hot cocoa, mix 2 Tbsp. of the mix with 1 cup of hot water. ¼ tsp. vanilla may also be added.

*Tastes best with higher quality baking cocoa.

Mexican Hot Chocolate

½   cup sugar
⅓   cup baking cocoa
1   tsp. ground cinnamon
½   tsp. salt
7   cups dairy free milk (rice, soy or coconut)
1   Tbsp. vanilla

Combine sugar, cocoa, cinnamon, and salt in a large saucepan. Slowly stir in milk and heat almost to boiling, simmer for 2 minutes.

Remove from heat and add vanilla. Beat until frothy with an electric mixer or whisk. Serve by garnishing with a cinnamon stick or a dollop of coconut milk whipped cream (p.310). Serves 6.

Orange Cinnamon Coffee

⅓   cup ground coffee
1½   tsp. orange peel, grated
½   tsp. cinnamon
½   tsp. vanilla

Blend coffee and dry ingredients in a blender. Blend in vanilla. Scrape sides and blend 15 seconds more. Brew. Makes one 8-cup pot of brewed coffee.

Spiced Tea

4 cups boiling water
4 tsp. loose black tea
6 whole cloves
½ tsp. dried orange peel
⅛ tsp. cinnamon

Mix all the ingredients in a teapot and pour boiling water on top. Let steep 3-5 minutes. Stir, strain, and serve. Serves 4.

Double Berry Tea

2 cups hot water
2 Tbsp. seedless raspberry or strawberry jam
3 blackberry tea bags
1 tsp. lemon juice
2 tsp. sugar

In a small saucepan, bring water and jam to a boil. Remove from heat and add tea bags. Steep 5 minutes covered. Remove tea bags and stir in lemon juice and sugar. Pour into tea cups and garnish with lemon twists. Serves 4.

- **To get the most juice from an orange, lemon, or lime, punch a couple of times with a fork. Microwave for 20 seconds, put into boiling water for 3-4 minutes. Or you can also try rolling on the counter with the palm of your hand.**

Sweet Tea

3   regular sized tea bags*
1½   qts. boiling water
½-¾   cup sugar

In a pitcher, combine tea bags, water and sugar. Let steep 10-20 minutes, depending on the desired strength. Stir well and chill.

Serve over ice cubes. This will be strong but when you put the ice cubes in, the tea will be the right strength.

Add a sprig of mint to your glasses. You can also try replacing 1 regular tea bag with a flavored tea bag for variety. Makes 1½ quarts.

*To make flavored tea, add a package of flavored drink mix to each pot of tea.

Wassail

8   cups apple cider
¼   cup brown sugar
1   tsp. whole cloves
1   tsp. whole allspice
1   cinnamon stick

Heat all the ingredients to boiling; reduce heat. Cover and simmer 20 minutes. Strain and pour into a punch bowl. Serves 8.

Real Lemonade

1   cup sugar
2   cups boiling water
5   large lemons*
3   cups water

In a 2 quart pitcher, add the sugar and boiling water. Stir until sugar is dissolved. Squeeze the juice from the lemons and remove seeds. Add to the sugar/water mix. Add the remaining 3 cups of water. Chill for 2-3 hours. You can adjust sugar and water to how sweet or strong you want it.

Limeade

Make the same as lemonade but use limes instead. Add maraschino cherry juice for cherry limeades.

Simple Limeade

1   can 7up
1   Tbsp. maraschino cherry juice
     crushed ice
     lime wedge

Pour the 7up, cherry juice, and ice into a cup. Add the lime wedge.

- **Make lemonade like this in the winter** and heat it up for a hot drink. This is especially good for when you have a cold.

- **For pink lemonade,** add a small amount of maraschino cherry juice.

- **For variations on your lemonade,** freeze things like watermelon juice, berry juice, berries, fruit purees or mint leaves in ice cube trays to add to your lemonade.

- **Place glasses in the freezer to chill.** Pour drinks into them on a hot day. Just looking at it will cool you down and will make the drink seem extra special, even if it is a simple glass of Kool-Aid.

Orange Slush

1	cup orange juice
1	Tbsp. honey
½	banana
4	ice cubes
1	tsp. vanilla (optional)

Blend all ingredients until smooth in a blender. Serves 1.

Creamy Orange Shake
(Tastes like Orange Julius)

⅓	cup frozen orange juice concentrate
½	cup coconut milk
¼	cup sugar
½	cup water
½	tsp. vanilla
5-6	ice cubes
2	scoops vanilla coconut milk ice cream (optional)

Combine ingredients in a blender until smooth. This can be kept in the refrigerator up to 1 day. Serves 4.

Banana Milkshake

3   bananas, frozen
4   cups dairy free milk (rice, soy or coconut)
1   tsp. vanilla
¼   cup sugar
6   crushed ice cubes

Place all the ingredients in a blender and blend until smooth. Serve immediately. Serves 4.

Other stir-ins:

- cocoa powder

- jams or jellies

- coconut

- other fruits

Fruit Slushie

6   cups water
4   cups sugar
5   bananas, mashed
1   (46 oz.) can pineapple juice
1   (6 oz.) small can frozen lemon juice
1   (6 oz.) small can frozen orange juice

Bring water and sugar to a boil. Boil 3-5 minutes. Cool. Add all the other ingredients to the water and sugar mixture. Freeze overnight. Put a scoop in a glass and pour lemon-lime soda on top. Serves 50.

Smoothies

2   cups fresh, frozen or canned fruit
2   cups dairy free milk (rice, soy or coconut) or 1 cup DF milk
      and 1 cup DF yogurt
1   cup ice cubes
3   Tbsp. sugar
1   tsp. vanilla

In a blender, combine all ingredients and blend until smooth.
Makes 2 smoothies.

You can make any combination of the following for your smoothies. When using juices, replace juice for milk in the recipe.

- Top off any smoothie with ginger ale or sparkling water.

- strawberries, blueberries, peaches, and a sprig of mint

- strawberries, blueberries, raspberries, and blackberries

- strawberries, raspberries, and banana

- orange juice, pineapple juice, banana

- crushed pineapple, ¼ tsp. coconut flavoring

- apple juice, coconut, and ¼ tsp. grated ginger

- banana and 2 Tbsp. peanut butter

- banana, strawberries, 2 Tbsp. chocolate syrup

- strawberries, banana, peaches, and apple

- ¼ tsp. mint extract, ¼ cup chocolate syrup

- ¼ cup chocolate syrup

- ⅓ cup unsweetened grape juice

- ¼ cup chocolate syrup and ¼ cup coffee (Don't use with fruit.)

Smoothies
(Continued)

Other Add-Ins

- ¼ cup gluten free oatmeal

- flax seed oil

- bee pollen

- breakfast powder (vegan)

- protein powder (vegan)

- instant coffee

- powdered soft drink mix

- 2 Tbsp. fruit juice concentrate

- cinnamon

- nutmeg

- any flavorings such as cherry, strawberry, peppermint, etc.

- whipped coconut cream

- bananas and kiwi fruit

- watermelon

- cantaloupe

- mixed berries and peaches or pears

- peaches and ¼ tsp. cinnamon

- **Use small juice glasses. ½ cup of juice is one serving of fruit.**

David's Punch

(My brother's favorite punch. We HAVE to have it every Christmas!)

1   qt. cranberry juice
2   lemons, squeezed, or 2 oz. lemon juice
1   pint orange juice
4   qts. ginger ale

Combine juices and chill. Pour into a punch bowl over a block of ice and add ginger ale. Garnish glasses with mint sprigs. Orange sherbet scoops may be added.

When making punch for a party, freeze part of it in a mold. Float the block of frozen punch in the punch bowl. This prevents diluting. Makes 44 servings.

- **Store lemons in a sealed jar of water in the refrigerator. You will be able to get more juice out of them.**

- **Combine 2 cups of flat soda with 1 package of unflavored gelatin to make a great flavored gelatin. This is particularly good with root beer, orange, and grape sodas.**

Chocolate Soda

2   Tbsp. chocolate syrup
½   cup club soda
1-2 large scoops dairy free vanilla ice cream

Mix chocolate syrup and club soda in a tall glass. Add ice cream. Pour in more soda. Stir to blend and serve at once. Serves 1.

Cherry Syrup

1   pkg. cherry flavored drink mix
1½ cups water
½   cup sugar

Stir ingredients together until sugar is dissolved. Keep refrigerated.

Add 2 to 3 tablespoons to your favorite glass of soda. Works especially well for lemon-lime soda and colas. Makes 2 cups.

Daily Prayer
O God, help me to keep my big mouth shut
until I know what I am talking about.

Breakfasts

Breakfast Tips

- **Add a pinch of salt to your oatmeal and grits.** It will bring out the sweetness of the sugar, so you use less.

- **Spread some peanut butter and honey** or corn syrup on a pancake and roll up for a snack. This is great for leftover pancakes.

- **Mix all the dry ingredients for pancakes** and muffins the night before. Mix all the wet ingredients and keep in the refrigerator. Then simply mix the two in the morning.

- **Make a double or triple batch of pancakes,** waffles or French toast on the weekend and freeze the leftovers. Put them in the toaster and they are ready to eat!

- **Mix cinnamon and sugar together** and keep in a shaker bottle. This works great for toast or when making cinnamon bread. An old spice bottle works great.

- **Compare the price of breakfast cereals by servings or portions and not by the ounce.** Cold cereal may be cheaper than oatmeal by the ounce but if you eat more per serving then it may actually cost more.

- **Whip a teaspoon of mayo into eggs BEFORE scrambling them.** They don't dry out that way. (It's hard to overcook eggs with a spoonful of mayo in them.) Eggs are very tasty this way! Use about a spoonful per 2 medium eggs. I've had people say "Yuck!" to this, until they tried it.

- **If muffins brown around the outside before the centers are cooked,** try partly filling one section of the muffin pan with water. The extra steam will keep the edges from cooking.

- **Lightly salt melons to bring out their sweetness.**

Cinnamon Streusel Coffee Cake

1½ cups gluten free baking mix*
½ cup sugar
2 eggs
½ cup dairy free milk (rice or soy)
1 tsp. vanilla

Streusel Topping

⅔ cup gluten free baking mix
2 Tbsp. dairy free butter, melted
½ cup brown sugar
1 tsp. cinnamon

Preheat oven to 350°. Grease a 9x9 inch cake pan. Combine ingredients for cake in a bowl and whisk until smooth. Spread into pan. Mix streusel topping and sprinkle top of cake with streusel gently pressing some down into cake mix.

Bake until cake tests clean with a toothpick or knife inserted into the center, about 22-26 minutes. Cool before cutting.

*My gluten free baking mix includes butter flavored shortening. If your baking mix does not have shortening in the mix, add ¼ cup shortening or melted dairy free butter.

Pancakes

1	cup gluten free all purpose flour
¼	tsp. xanthan gum (if not in flour)
1	Tbsp. baking powder
¼	tsp. salt
2	Tbsp. sugar
2	Tbsp. vegetable oil
1	egg
1	tsp. vanilla
¾	cup dairy free milk (rice or soy)

In a bowl, mix the dry ingredients. Add wet ingredients and mix until combined. The mixture will be thick and lumpy. For thinner pancakes add 1-2 Tbsp. more milk.

Heat a griddle or frying pan over medium heat and lightly grease. Cook on a hot greased griddle. Flip when bubbles break on the surface and edges begin to dry. Makes 15-18 pancakes.

Stir any of the following into pancakes for an added treat or for more nutrition:

- blueberries or chopped apples

- bacon

- nuts

- cinnamon

- dairy free chocolate chips

Waffles

2	eggs
2	cups gluten free all purpose flour
¼	tsp. xanthan gum (if not in flour)
2	Tbsp. sugar
½	cup vegetable oil or dairy free butter, melted
4	tsp. baking powder
¼	tsp. salt
1¾	cups dairy free milk (rice or soy)
½	tsp. vanilla

Heat waffle iron. Beat eggs in a medium bowl until fluffy. Beat in remaining ingredients, just until smooth. Do not over mix. Pour batter onto center of hot waffle iron. Bake 5 minutes or until the steaming stops. Remove carefully.

Stir any of the following into waffle batter for an added treat or for more nutrition:

- blueberries or chopped apples

- bacon

- nuts

- cinnamon

- dairy free chocolate chips

A waffle is like a more considerate pancake.
It is like, "Here let me hold the syrup for you
in these little boxes."

French Toast

1   egg, slightly beaten
1½   cups dairy free milk (rice or soy)
1   Tbsp. sugar
½   tsp. vanilla
¼   tsp salt
½   tsp. cinnamon
10-12 slices gluten free bread

Put egg in a shallow dish and beat. Mix in milk, sugar, vanilla, salt and cinnamon. Heat griddle over medium heat and grease. Dip bread slices into egg mixture and cook on each side until golden brown. Serve with syrup or powdered sugar and dairy free butter. Makes 10-12 slices.

- **Day-old or dried out bread works best.** If you don't have day-old bread, lightly toast the bread and then dip in the batter so it doesn't get soggy.

- **French toast tastes great fried in bacon grease.**

French Toast Sticks

After cooking French toast, cut each piece into 4 strips. Kids love to dip these in syrup.

Banana French Toast

In a blender, combine all the ingredients for French toast except bread with 1 ripe banana. Blend until smooth. Use as you would regular French toast batter.

- **Put powdered sugar in a spice bottle to sprinkle on cakes and French toast.**

Gluten Free Baking Mix

2⅔   cups tapioca flour
1⅓   cups potato starch
1⅓   cups corn starch
1⅓   cups brown or white rice flour
1⅓   cups sweet white rice flour
2   tsp. xanthan gum
2   Tbsp. baking powder
2   tsp. salt

Mix well. Makes 8 cups.

Half Batch GF Baking Mix

1⅓   cup tapioca flour
⅔   cup potato starch
⅔   cup corn starch
⅔   cup brown or white rice flour
⅔   cup sweet white rice flour
1   Tbsp. baking powder
1   tsp. xanthan gum
1   tsp. salt

Mix well. Makes 4 cups.

Baking Mix

(Without Cornstarch)

2 cups brown rice flour
1 cup white rice flour
1 cup tapioca starch
1 cup potato starch
½ cup sugar
3 Tbsp. baking powder
2 tsp. xanthan gum
2 tsp. salt
1 cup butter flavored shortening

Mix the dry ingredients. Cut in shortening. Use a mixer on low to cut in the shortening to save time. Store in an airtight container up to 6 months.

Baking Mix Pancakes

2¼ cups baking mix (see above)
¼ cup sugar
1 egg
1½ cups water
2 Tbsp. vegetable oil

Mix ingredients until moist. The batter should be lumpy. Cook on a hot greased griddle. Flip when bubbles break on the surface and the edges begin to dry.

Makes 15-18 medium pancakes.

Baking Mix Biscuits

2¼ cups gluten free baking mix (p.54-55)
⅔ cup water or dairy free milk (rice or soy)

Preheat oven to 450°. Mix lightly until dough forms a ball. Turn onto a lightly floured surface. Knead 10-12 times. Roll dough about ½ inch thick. Cut with a 2 inch cutter or the rim of a glass dipped in gluten free flour. Bake 10-12 minutes on an ungreased cookie sheet.

For drop biscuits, use 1 cup water and drop by tablespoons full onto a baking sheet. Makes one dozen.

*For cheese biscuits, add ¼ cup shredded dairy free Cheddar cheese.

Baking Mix Muffins

2¼ cups gluten free baking mix (p.54-55)
¼ cup sugar
1 egg
¾ cup water
⅓ cup vegetable oil

Preheat oven to 400°. Mix dry baking mix and sugar. Add egg, water and vegetable oil to dry ingredients. Mix only enough to moisten baking mix. The batter will be lumpy. Fill greased muffin tins ⅔ full. Bake
20 minutes.

*For an added surprise, fill muffin cup half way and then add a spoonful of jelly. Top with more batter. Add raisins, cinnamon or nuts for gourmet muffins. Makes 12-15 muffins.

- **If you don't have a biscuit cutter or cookie cutter, use the ring from a canning jar.**

Muffins

3   eggs
¾   cup dairy free milk (rice or soy)
1   Tbsp. vinegar
½   cup butter flavored shortening or dairy free butter,
       melted and cooled
1   tsp. vanilla
2   cups gluten free all purpose flour
1   tsp. xanthan gum (if not in flour)
1   tsp. baking powder
½   tsp. baking soda
½   tsp. salt
½   cup sugar
¼   cup light brown sugar, packed
½-1 cup mix-ins (one or a combination, optional)
       chocolate chips, raisins, chopped nuts, chopped apples

Crumb Topping

4   Tbsp. dairy free butter, melted
½   cup light brown sugar, packed
½   cup gluten free all purpose flour
¼   tsp. xanthan gum (if not in flour)
⅛   tsp. salt

Preheat oven to 350°. Grease or line muffin tin. Place eggs, milk, vinegar, shortening and vanilla into a medium size bowl. Mix well. Add the rest of the ingredients. Mix well, but don't over mix. Add mix-ins, if desired, and combine.

Divide evenly into muffin tins. If you are adding the crumb topping, sprinkle generously on the top of the muffin batter and press to adhere the mixture to the muffin batter. Bake 20 minutes. If you are including the crumb topping, the muffins may take another minute or so to bake fully. Remove from the oven and allow the muffins to cool completely.

Jam Muffins

Fill greased muffin cups ¼ full. Place 1 tsp. jam on top of the batter and fill with more batter until the muffin cup is ⅔ full.

Cinnamon Roll Muffins

1½   cups gluten free all purpose flour
¾   tsp. xanthan gum (if not in flour)
⅛   tsp. salt
½   cup sugar
2   tsp. baking powder
¾   cups dairy free milk (almond or coconut)
1   egg
1   tsp. vanilla
¼   cup butter flavored shortening or dairy free butter, melted

Topping

¼   cup dairy free butter, softened
¼   cup brown sugar, packed
½   Tbsp. gluten free all purpose flour
¾   tsp. cinnamon

Preheat oven to 350°. Use cupcake liners or spray a with muffin pan with cooking spray.

In a bowl, add flour, xanthan gum (if using), salt, sugar, baking powder, milk, egg and vanilla. Mix until fully combined. Stir in the shortening.

Mix topping ingredients. Drop by spoonfuls around batter in bowl. Gently fold topping into batter without mixing. Fill greased muffin cups ⅔ full of batter. Bake 24-26 minutes. Use a toothpick to check and see if the centers are done.

Glaze

1   cup powdered sugar
2   Tbsp. dairy free milk (any DF milk)
½   tsp. vanilla

In a medium bowl, whisk the powdered sugar, milk and vanilla together. Drizzle over the warm muffin.

Oatmeal Muffins

1	cup gluten free oats
½	cup brown sugar, packed
1	cup gluten free all purpose flour
1	tsp. xanthan gum (if not in flour)
1	tsp. baking powder
½	tsp. salt
½	tsp. baking soda
½	tsp. cinnamon (optional)
1	cup dairy free milk (rice or soy)
1	tsp. vinegar
1	egg
½	cup vegetable oil
1	cup raisins (optional)

Preheat oven to 400°. Mix all ingredients in the order listed. The batter will be lumpy. Spoon batter into greased muffin tins ⅔ full.

Bake 15-20 minutes. Makes 1 dozen.

The best sellers in many bookstores
are cookbooks and diet books.
One tells you how to prepare your food...
the other tells you how not to eat it!

Apple Cinnamon Muffins

2   cups gluten free all purpose flour
1   tsp. xanthan gum (if not in flour)
1   tsp. ground cinnamon
1   tsp. baking powder
½   tsp. baking soda
¼   tsp. salt
½   cup raisins and/or nuts
1   cup apple juice
½   cup applesauce
2   Tbsp. oil
½   cup raisins and/or nuts (optional)

Topping

3   Tbsp. sugar
¼   tsp. nutmeg
¼   tsp. cinnamon
    dairy free butter, melted

Preheat oven to 350°. Combine muffin ingredients and mix. Spoon into lightly greased muffin tins. Bake 20-25 minutes, until toothpick inserted in center comes out clean.

Mix sugar, nutmeg and cinnamon to make topping.

While muffins are still warm, dip tops in melted butter and then topping. Makes 12-15 muffins.

Scrambled Eggs

8   eggs
1   tsp. salt
¼   tsp. pepper
4   Tbsp. water (optional)
4   tsp. dairy free butter or bacon grease

Stir all the ingredients except butter or bacon grease in a bowl until well blended. Heat a skillet on medium heat. Add butter or bacon grease. Pour egg mixture into skillet. Stir constantly, about 4 minutes, until eggs are fluffy and set. Serves 4.

Poached Eggs

4   eggs
     water

In a large saucepan, heat water to boiling. Reduce to a simmer. Break each egg into a cup. Hold the cup over the water and gently slip the egg into the water. Cook 3 minutes, until whites are set.

Remove the eggs with a slotted spoon and allow to drain briefly. Serve on buttered toast or English muffins. Serves 4.

- **To test eggs for freshness: Place an egg in a glass of cold water. If it floats, do not use it.**

- **Save your bacon grease. Use it for frying eggs, flavoring cornbread or muffins or for greasing pans.**

- **When frying bacon, sprinkle a little sugar in the skillet. Your bacon won't stick to the pan.**

Broiled Grapefruit

2   grapefruit
2   Tbsp. brown sugar
½   tsp. cinnamon
1   Tbsp. dairy free butter

Cut grapefruit in half. Mix cinnamon and brown sugar. Sprinkle a little on each grapefruit. Dot a little bit of dairy free butter on top of the brown sugar and cinnamon. Broil 10 minutes. Serve warm. Serves 4.

Cantaloupe Balls

1   cantaloupe
¼ -½ cup sugar
¼ -½ cup corn syrup

Halve and seed cantaloupe. Then scoop out the flesh with a melon baller or cut into chunks. Add corn syrup and sugar, to taste. Let sit in the refrigerator overnight. Serves 4-6.

Applesauce

5   lbs. apples, peeled, cored and chopped
2   cups water
1½ cups sugar
¼   tsp. each salt, cloves, nutmeg
½   tsp. cinnamon
1   tsp. vanilla

Mix everything but vanilla in a saucepan and boil until apples are tender. Add vanilla. Serve warm or chilled. Serves 8.

Rice Cereal

2   cups leftover rice
½   tsp. cinnamon
2   Tbsp. sugar
2   cups dairy free milk (rice or soy)
1   tsp. dairy free butter

Combine all the ingredients in a saucepan. Cook on medium heat until warmed, but not boiling. You can adjust the cinnamon and sugar to your taste. This can also be microwaved very easily. Serves 4.

Millet

Presoaking

1   cup millet
3   cups water for soaking
½   cup water for cooking
½   tsp. salt

Combine millet and water and soak for at least 7-8 hours. Drain in a colander and rinse well. In a medium saucepan, combine soaked millet, water and salt. Bring to a boil and cover the pot. Reduce the temperature to low and simmer 10-20 minutes.

No Presoaking

1   cup millet
2   cups water
½   tsp. salt

In a medium saucepan, combine millet, water and salt. Bring to a boil and cover. Reduce the temperature to low and simmer 30 minutes.

Oatmeal Ideas

Cook gluten free oatmeal according to the instructions on the package.

Stir any of the following into oatmeal:

- sugar
- applesauce
- cinnamon and sugar
- chopped fruit
- brown sugar
- dried apples
- raisins
- molasses
- berries

- maple syrup
- bananas
- jam or jelly
- chopped peaches
- plain or fruit yogurt
- honey
- dark brown sugar and 1 drop of maple extract makes oatmeal taste just like the store bought instant oatmeal.

- **Melt peanut butter in hot oatmeal and top with chocolate chips.**

- **Present oatmeal in a fancy glass such as a sundae dish. Sprinkle granola, fruit, honey, brown sugar, or nuts on top.**

Overnight Oats

½ cup almond milk
¾ Tbsp. chia seeds
2 Tbsp. peanut butter (creamy or crunchy) (optional)
1 Tbsp. brown sugar
½ cup gluten free oatmeal

Toppings

Top with any of the following (optional):

- sliced bananas

- strawberries

- raspberries

- flaxseed meal

- chia seeds

- gluten free granola

In a mason jar or small bowl, add almond milk, chia seeds, peanut butter and brown sugar. Stir with a spoon to combine. The peanut butter doesn't need to be completely mixed with the milk.

Add oats and stir a few more times. Then press down with a spoon to ensure all oats have been moistened and are immersed in milk.

Cover securely with a lid or plastic wrap and set in the refrigerator overnight (or for at least 6 hours).

The next day, open and enjoy as is or garnish with desired toppings (see options above).

Overnight oats will keep in the refrigerator up to 2 days, though they're best within the first 12-24 hours.

Granola

¾   cup brown sugar
⅓   cup vegetable oil
⅓   cup honey
5   cups gluten free oatmeal
¾   tsp. cinnamon
     pinch of salt
½   cup raisins

Preheat oven to 375°. Mix brown sugar, oil and honey in a saucepan. Bring to a boil and heat until the brown sugar is dissolved. Combine dry ingredients in a large cake pan. Pour syrup over dry mixture and mix well.

Bake 10 minutes. Stir occasionally. Let cool in pan. Add raisins and stir. Store in an airtight container.

You can also add coconut, nuts, dates and other dried fruit. Makes 5 cups.

Fruit Flavored Syrup

2   cups water
¾   cup sugar
1   pkg. flavored drink mix (strawberry or cherry are great)
2   Tbsp. cornstarch

Mix ingredients and bring to a boil while stirring. Boil several minutes to thicken. Pour into a pitcher and serve hot. Makes 2 cups.

This syrup can be used to flavor milk or poured over pancakes and waffles.

Maple Syrup

1   cup water
2   cups sugar
¼   tsp. maple flavoring
1   Tbsp. dairy free butter

Stir first three ingredients together. Bring to a boil. Simmer for
2-3 minutes. Add butter, stir and cool. Pour into a serving container.
Makes 1 pint.

Honey Syrup

½   cup water
1   cup honey
1   tsp. vanilla

Heat water in a saucepan over medium heat. Add honey just before
boiling. Stir well until combined. Do not boil. Remove from heat and
stir in vanilla. Store, covered, in the refrigerator.

Honey can be used straight from the jar on pancakes, however this
syrup pours nicely and dilutes the overwhelming sweetness of honey.
Makes 1 cup.

- **When you need to measure honey or corn syrup, oil the measuring cup first. Then the honey will pour out easily.**

Notes

Breads

Gluten Free Bread Baking Tips

READ ALL INSTRUCTIONS BEFORE MAKING GLUTEN FREE BREAD!!!!!

Follow the recipe exactly before experimenting: If you've never made gluten free bread before, gluten free dough is going to be much wetter than a regular dough. **FOLLOW THE RECIPE EXACTLY!** Don't add additional flour or you'll end up with a brick.

Not all gluten free all purpose flours are the same: I tested all of these recipes with Great Value gluten free all purpose flour mix (Walmart) and King Arthur gluten free all purpose flour mix.

If you use any other gluten free all purpose flour mix, be sure to read the ingredients. Most (but not all) can be substituted 1 for 1 in place of regular flour when baking gluten free.

Xanthan gum is a filler that helps give bread its "springiness" and makes it thicker. It is the ingredient that replaces the gluten in gluten free recipes. Use **ONLY** the amount recommended and **DO NOT** add more if your gluten free all purpose flour mix already has xanthan gum in it.

If your gluten free all purpose flour DOES NOT have xanthan gum in it, you can add it in the following amounts:

- **Bread and Pizza Dough:** 1 tsp. xanthan gum per cup of gluten free all purpose flour

- **Cakes, Muffins and Quick Breads:** ½ tsp. xanthan gum per cup of gluten free all purpose flour

- **Cookie and Bar Cookies:** ½ tsp. xanthan gum per cup of gluten free all purpose flour

Baking Powder AND yeast together? Yes, in gluten free baking you need both to replace the gluten and have your breads rise like "regular" bread.

Baking Powder: Make sure the one you are using is gluten free.

Apple Cider Vinegar is used to tenderize the dough and make it more like "real" bread. **DO NOT leave this out.** It is what makes your gluten free bread go from just "ok" to "Wow! This is great!"

Dairy Free Milks: I include in parentheses with each recipe which dairy free milks I used to test the recipe. You can pretty much use any dairy free milk you want but some, like coconut and almond, sometimes change the taste of baked goods and make the flavor seem "off", while rice and soy have a more "neutral" taste.

Room Temperature Ingredients: Make sure all ingredients are at room temperature (including the flour, eggs and yeast). If everything but your eggs are at room temperature, you can put the eggs in some very hot, but not boiling, water for 3-5 minutes to warm up.

Use the mixer paddle attachment (flat beater): When mixing gluten free bread dough in a stand mixer, use the paddle and not the whisk attachment or bread hook. Gluten free bread requires no kneading so no bread hook is required. If using a regular mixer, the regular beaters will work fine.

Use a meat thermometer: To double check that yeast bread or rolls are finished baking, use an instant read meat thermometer to check the internal temperature. A perfectly baked yeast loaf will reach an internal temperature of 202-205 degrees or 200 degrees at high altitude.

Can I substitute (fill in the blank)? These recipes were tested as they are written and they work **IF** you follow the directions **EXACTLY!** Feel free to substitute anything you want but the results may or may not work out.

I strongly recommend making a recipe exactly according to the recipe the first time before attempting substitutions.

Always bake on the middle rack in your oven!

Alway preheat your oven!

Gluten Free Flour Mix

2⅔ cups tapioca flour
1⅓ cups potato starch
1⅓ cups corn starch
1⅓ cups brown or white rice flour
1⅓ cups sweet white rice flour
2   tsp. xanthan gum

Mix everything well. Makes 8 cups.

Sometimes I wish someone would just
hug me and say,
I know it is hard but you will be ok
and hand me a coffee
and five million dollars.

No Knead Gluten Free Bread

3   cups gluten free all purpose flour
1   tsp. active dry yeast
1   tsp. xanthan gum (if not in flour)
1   tsp. salt (optional - I used Himalayan salt.)
1   cup water

Mix everything together but the water. Then add water slowly. Once everything is well combined, let rest for 3 hours.

After 3 hours, place the dough on a floured surface and roll into a ball. Place rolled dough in a bowl lined with parchment paper and cover with a cloth for 30 minutes.

Place empty Dutch oven, covered with the lid, into the oven. Turn on the oven to 450°. Once the oven reaches 450°, remove Dutch oven and carefully place rolled dough inside. Cover, return to oven and let bake for 30 minutes.

After 30 minutes, remove lid from Dutch oven and continue baking, uncovered, for 10-15 more minutes.

Remove from oven. Let sit for 10-15 minutes and serve.

• **Reuse aluminum foil. To store, flatten and save in a file folder.**

GF DF
Sandwich Bread

using store bought flour

Tested with Walmart Great Value Gluten Free Flour Mix and
Bob's Red Mill Gluten Free Flour Mix.

1¾   cups warm water (100°)
3   tsp. active dry yeast (not instant yeast)
2   Tbsp. + 2 tsp. sugar or honey

3⅔   cups gluten free all purpose flour
1   Tbsp. baking powder (high altitude, use 2½ tsp.)
1   tsp. salt
1   egg
⅓   cup shortening, melted

Place water, yeast and sugar in a bowl. Whisk well until yeast is dissolved. Then let it sit until foamy, about 5 minutes. Add remaining ingredients.

Combine the bread dough thoroughly until smooth, either with an electric mixer or vigorously by hand, using a large whisk, until there are no lumps remaining at all.

Pour dough into a greased 9x5x3 inch bread pan. (Note: DO NOT use an 8x4 inch pan.)

Set dough in a warm place until it has risen to ¼ inch below the top of the bread pan, about 15 minutes. (DO NOT let it rise higher than ¼ inch below the top.)

Preheat oven to 375°.

Place the bread pan with the dough into the oven on the center rack. Bake 40-55 minutes. When baked, the bread will be golden brown and have an internal temperature between 200°-205° or a skewer pushed inside will come out mostly clean with just a *slight* amount of sticky dough on the end.

Remove the bread from the oven and let it cool in the pan 5 minutes. Then carefully transfer the loaf to a cooling rack, laying on its side to cool.

Let the bread cool for one hour before slicing.

Store in a plastic bag or airtight container at room temperature for up to 5 days. Slice and freeze if necessary.

This bread can be frozen once it is completely cooled. Wrap the loaf tightly in plastic wrap. Then wrap it in foil or freezer paper. Place the wrapped loaf in a freezer bag. The bread can be frozen up to 3 months. When ready to use, thaw in the refrigerator overnight.

Herbed Bread

Add 6 tablespoons fresh herbs to flour. Chives, sage and thyme work well.

Jalapeno Cheddar Bread

Add ½-1 cup dairy free Cheddar cheese and ¼ -½ cup chopped jalapenos.

GF DF
Sandwich Bread

using homemade GF flours

1¾	cups warm water (100°)
3	tsp. active dry yeast (not instant yeast)
2	Tbsp. + 2 tsp. sugar or honey
1⅓	cups tapioca flour
⅔	cup potato starch
⅔	cup cornstarch
⅔	cup brown or white rice flour
⅔	cup sweet white rice flour
1	Tbsp. baking powder (high altitude, use 2½ tsp.)
1	tsp. xanthan gum
1	tsp. salt
1	egg
⅓	cup shortening, melted

Place water, yeast and sugar in a bowl. Whisk well until yeast is dissolved. Then let it sit until foamy, about 5 minutes. Add remaining ingredients.

Combine the bread dough thoroughly until smooth, either with an electric mixer or vigorously by hand, using a large whisk, until there are no lumps remaining at all.

Pour dough into a greased 9x5x3 inch bread pan. (Note: DO NOT use an 8x4 inch pan.)

Set dough in a warm place until it has risen to ¼ inch below the top of the bread pan, about 15 minutes. (DO NOT let it rise higher than ¼ inch below the top.)

Preheat oven to 375°.

Place the bread pan with the dough into the oven on the center rack. Bake 40-55 minutes. When baked, the bread will be golden brown and have an internal temperature between 200°-205° or a skewer pushed inside will come out mostly clean with just a *slight* amount of sticky dough on the end.

Remove the bread from the oven and let it cool in the pan 5 minutes. Then carefully transfer the loaf to a cooling rack, laying on its side to cool.

Let the bread cool for one hour before slicing.

Store in a plastic bag or airtight container at room temperature for up to 5 days. Slice and freeze if necessary.

This bread can be frozen once it is completely cooled. Wrap the loaf tightly in plastic wrap. Then wrap it in foil or freezer paper. Place the wrapped loaf in a freezer bag. The bread can be frozen up to 3 months. When ready to use, thaw in the refrigerator overnight.

Herbed Bread

Add 6 tablespoons fresh herbs to flour. Chives, sage and thyme work well.

Jalapeno Cheddar Bread

Add ½-1 cup dairy free Cheddar cheese and ¼ -½ cup chopped jalapenos.

- **To check to see if the baking powder in your pantry is still active, stir one teaspoon into ⅓ cup hot water. There should be immediate vigorous bubbling. If no bubbling occurs or bubbling is sporadic, the baking powder is past its prime.**

Troubleshooting GF DF Bread

Here are some problems some people encounter making GF DF bread, along with how to deal with them:

My bread overflowed and made a huge mess. You **CAN NOT** let your bread rise higher than 1 inch below the top of the pan. If you do, it will overflow. If it does overflow, it may still be edible so, if possible, place a baking sheet under it and let it finish cooking.

Also MAKE SURE your bread pan is 9x5 inch and NOT 8x4 inch.

My bread is flat. Make sure your pan is 9x5 inches. This is the pan that works the best to make the most "normal" loaf of bread.

My bread didn't rise. Either your yeast is dead or not fresh or your water wasn't hot enough. Use a thermometer to make sure your water is the right temperature and buy fresh yeast.

The bread fell in the middle. You let it rise too high and then it fell when cooling OR you slammed the oven door or jarred the bread while baking in some way and it fell. **DO NOT OPEN THE DOOR** to the oven until your bread has cooked **AT LEAST** 40 minutes.

My bread is undercooked in the middle. Use a meat thermometer to stick into the bread and make sure the temperature is **AT LEAST** 200° before removing from the oven. If the top is getting too brown and you need to let it cook more, place a piece of foil over the top to stop the browning.

I want to substitute (fill in the blank). These recipes were tested as written and work IF you follow the directions **EXACTLY!** Feel free to substitute anything you want, but the results may or may not work out.

I just can't get this bread to work. I tested more than 25 loaves of gluten free dairy free bread. This **IS** the easiest and most delicious gluten free dairy free bread. If it is not working, try making it at least 5 times, paying careful attention to the instructions, to see if you can get it to work. It **REALLY** is **MUCH** cheaper ($1.50) than the store bought bread and **MUCH** tastier, so it **IS** worth learning how to make it.

French Bread

2   cups white rice flour
1   cup tapioca flour
3   tsp. xanthan gum
1½ tsp. salt
2   Tbsp. sugar
2   Tbsp. rapid rise yeast
1½ cups warm water (110°)
2   Tbsp. dairy free butter, melted
3   egg whites, beaten slightly
1   tsp. vinegar
     melted dairy free butter, for brushing (optional)

In a bowl, add flours, xanthan gum (if using) and salt. Blend with a mixer on low.

In a separate small bowl, dissolve the sugar and yeast in the water. Wait until the mixture foams slightly, then blend into the dry ingredients. Add butter, egg whites and vinegar. Beat on high for 3 minutes.

Grease 2 cookie sheets and dust with cornmeal.

To form loaves, spoon dough onto cookie sheets in two long French loaf shapes or spoon into special French bread pans. Slash diagonally every few inches. If desired, brush with melted butter.

Preheat oven to 400°.

Cover the dough and let rise (out of the oven) in a warm place until doubled in bulk, about 20 to 25 minutes. Bake 40 to 45 minutes. Remove from pan to cool.

Garlic Bread

Spread dairy free garlic butter (p.342) onto bread. Broil until golden brown.

Dinner Rolls

2½   cups gluten free all purpose flour
¼   cup sugar
2¼   tsp. (1 pkg.) instant yeast
1   tsp. salt
1   cup warm water (110°)
3   Tbsp. butter flavored shortening or dairy free butter,
        melted and cooled
1   egg
1   tsp. apple cider vinegar

Combine flour, sugar, yeast and salt in a mixing bowl. Add water, shortening, egg and apple cider vinegar using a mixer on low speed. Beat on medium speed for 3 minutes.

Grease an 8 inch round pan and scoop 9 mounds of dough, equally divided, into the pan. Wet your fingertips with water and smooth out the tops of rolls. Cover and let rise 45 minutes.

30 minutes into the rising time, preheat oven to 400°.

After rising, bake 20-25 minutes, until the tops are golden brown and the internal temperature is 200°-205°. Brush tops of rolls with dairy free butter.

Hamburger Buns

Starting with dinner roll recipe dough, scoop 4-5 mounds of dough, equally divided, onto a greased cookie sheet. Wet your fingertips with water and smooth out the tops of buns. Cover and let rise 45 minutes.

30 minutes into the rising time, preheat oven to 400°.

After rising, bake 20-25 minutes until the tops are golden brown and the internal temperature is 200°-205°. Brush tops of buns with dairy free butter.

Cornbread

2   cups gluten free all purpose flour
½   cup cornmeal
½   cup sugar
½   cup butter flavored shortening or dairy free butter, melted
1   tsp. baking powder
2   eggs
1   cup dairy free milk (rice or soy)

Preheat oven to 350°. In a large bowl, stir all the ingredients together. Blend until smooth. Pour into a greased 8x8 inch baking pan and bake for 30 minutes. Serves 9.

Be careful how you live.
You may be
the only Bible some people read.

Sourdough Bread Starter

Starter

1   pkg. or 1 Tbsp. yeast
1   cup warm water (110°-115°)
½   cup sugar
3   Tbsp. instant potato flakes

To make the starter:

Mix the starter ingredients in a glass jar or container. Cover loosely and let stand 24 hours at room temperature.

Put it in the refrigerator for three to five days.

On the fourth day, feed it with ½ cup sugar, 3 tablespoons potato flakes and 1 cup water. Stir and keep at room temperature for 24 hours.

You will use 1 cup of the starter to make the bread. Store the remaining starter in the refrigerator and feed it every 4 days. (If you don't make bread, discard 1 cup starter at each feeding.)

Never be discouraged.
Remember, Noah was an amateur.
The experts built the Titanic.

Sourdough Bread

2½ cups gluten free all purpose flour
1   tsp. xanthan gum (if not in flour)
1   tsp. baking powder
1   tsp. rapid rise/instant yeast
1   tsp. salt
¼   cup oil
¼   cup sugar or honey
1   tsp. apple cider vinegar
3   egg whites, room temperature
1   cup sourdough starter, room temperature
½   cups warm water (100-110°)

Spray a 9x5 inch bread pan with cooking spray. Preheat oven to 350°. Add flour, xanthan gum (if using), baking powder, instant yeast and salt to a large bowl and stir to combine the ingredients. Add oil, sugar, apple cider vinegar, egg whites, sourdough starter and warm water to the flour mixture and mix on low for 1 minute. If you are using a stand mixer, use the paddle attachment, not the dough hook. Mix on medium for 1 minute. The dough will look like a thick cake batter.

Pour the dough into the greased 9x5 inch bread pan. Spray top of loaf with cooking spray. Cover the top of the pan and allow to rise in a warm place for 30 minutes.

DO NOT ALLOW TO RISE MORE THAN 1 INCH BELOW THE TOP OF THE PAN.

Place in the oven and bake 30 minutes. Bake on the middle rack horizontally. When baked, it will be golden brown and have an internal temperature between 205° - 210° (high altitude 200°-205°).

The internal temperature MUST BE at LEAST 205°. If it is not and the top is getting too brown, put foil over the top and continue to bake another 10-15 minutes. Remove from the oven.

Let cool 10 minutes in pan and then remove from pan. If the bread cools in the pan, the steam can get trapped and the loaf can get soggy, especially on the bottom. Allow the bread to **COMPLETELY** cool before slicing.

Once cooled, store leftover bread in an airtight container. It may be kept on the counter at room temperature. It is best not to pre-slice the bread before you store it. Just store the leftover portion of the loaf.

This bread can be frozen once it is completely cooled. Wrap the loaf tightly in plastic wrap, then wrap it in foil or freezer paper. Place the wrapped loaf in a freezer bag. The bread can be frozen up to 3 months. Thaw the bread in the refrigerator overnight.

Herbed Bread

Add 6 tablespoons fresh herbs to flour. Chives, sage and thyme work well.

Jalapeno Cheddar Bread

Add ½-1 cup dairy free Cheddar cheese and ¼ -½ cup chopped jalapenos.

- **When cutting bread,** freeze the crumbs in a freezer bag. Use when a recipe calls for bread crumbs.

Hush Puppies

1½ cups cornmeal
½ cup gluten free all purpose flour
2 tsp. baking powder
½ tsp. salt
1 egg, well beaten
¾ cup dairy free milk (rice or soy)
1 small onion, grated or 1 tsp. onion powder
  dash Tabasco sauce (optional)
  vegetable oil for frying

Heat oil over medium heat to 375°.

Mix together cornmeal, flour, baking powder and salt in a bowl. In another bowl, mix the egg, milk, onion, and Tabasco sauce. Combine with dry ingredients.

Drop a teaspoonful at a time into the hot oil. When the hush puppies are crisp and golden (about 1 minute), remove from oil and drain on a paper towel. Serve hot. Serves 4-6.

Face powder may catch a man
but baking powder will keep him!

Biscuits

2   cups gluten free all purpose flour
1   tsp. xanthan gum (if not in flour)
¼   cup cornstarch
1   Tbsp. baking powder
½   tsp. salt
½   cup dairy free butter or shortening
1   cup dairy free milk (rice or soy), chilled
1   tsp. vinegar

Preheat oven to 375°. In a bowl, place flour, xanthan gum (if using), cornstarch, baking powder and salt. Whisk to combine well. Add butter. With fingertips, mix in flour mix to make "crumbs".

Create a well in the center of the dry ingredients and add milk and vinegar. Mix gently, just until the dough begins to come together. Divide the dough into 10 equal pieces. Roll each gently into a ball. Flatten lightly, about ¾ inch thick, and place about 2 inches apart on a greased baking sheet. Place the biscuits in the freezer to chill until firm (about 10 minutes).

Bake 20 minutes. For a more crisp bottom, allow the biscuits to bake for 2 to 3 minutes longer. Remove from the oven and allow to cool for 5 minutes before transferring to a wire rack to cool completely.

Garlic Cheese Biscuits

6   oz. dairy free cheddar cheese, grated
1   tsp. garlic powder
2   Tbsp. parsley, chopped

Add in with dry ingredients before adding butter.

- **To make biscuits in a hurry, pat or roll the dough into a rectangle and cut out square biscuits with a pizza cutter. This way the dough only needs to be rolled out once.**

Crepes

¾   cup dairy free milk (rice or soy)
½   cup water
2   eggs
1   cup gluten free all purpose flour
2   Tbsp. sugar
½   tsp. baking powder
½   tsp. salt
1   tsp. vanilla
3   Tbsp. dairy free butter, melted

Toppings

jelly
coconut whipped cream (p.310)

Mix ingredients. Beat until smooth. Heat a pan as you would for pancakes.

For each crepe, pour a scant ¼ cup of the batter into the skillet. Immediately rotate the skillet until a thin film covers bottom. Cook until light brown and bubbles pop on top. Turn with a spatula and cook the other side until light brown. (More often than not the first one doesn't turn out, but the others should be fine.)

Spread some of your favorite jelly or fresh fruit on each crepe. Roll and top with whipped topping. Makes 12 crepes.

•   **Save and freeze dried bread slices and heels. When you need bread crumbs, grind them in the blender or food processor. Toss with seasonings and melted dairy free butter or use in stuffing, croutons, or bread pudding.**

Coffee Cake

2   cups gluten free all purpose flour
1   tsp. xanthan gum (if not in flour)
2   tsp. baking powder
1   tsp. salt
¾   cup sugar
2   rounded Tbsp. shortening
1   cup dairy free milk (rice or soy)

Preheat oven to 350°. In a bowl, mix the flour, xanthan gum (if using), baking powder, salt, sugar, and shortening. Set aside ¾ cup of the mixture for the topping. Add the milk to the remainder of the flour mixture and mix until smooth.

Pour batter into an 8x8 inch greased pan and sprinkle topping over the top. Bake 30 minutes. Serves 9.

Topping

2   Tbsp. dairy free butter, melted
½   tsp. cinnamon
3   Tbsp. brown sugar
¾   cup mixture from above

Combine all ingredients for the topping with the flour mixture that was set aside and mix well.

- **If you need to measure 1 cup of shortening, fill a 2 cup measuring cup with 1 cup of water. Then spoon in shortening until the water level reaches 2 cups. Pour off water and you have exactly 1 cup of shortening.**

Apple Bread

1   egg
½   cup dairy free milk (rice or soy)
¼   cup applesauce
1½ cups gluten free all purpose flour
1   tsp. xanthan gum (if not in flour)
½   cup sugar
2   tsp. baking powder
½   tsp. cinnamon
1   cup apples, peeled, cored and diced

Topping

⅓   cup brown sugar
½   tsp. cinnamon

Preheat oven to 375°. Mix bread ingredients. Batter will be lumpy. Pour into a greased loaf pan floured with gluten free flour.

Mix topping ingredients and crumble over the top of mixture.

Bake 55-75 minutes. When done, a toothpick or knife stuck in the center should come out clean. Makes 1 loaf or 12-15 muffins.

For Muffins: Bake in greased muffin tins at 400° for 30-35 minutes.

One reason computers do so much work:

They don't have to stop and answer the phone.

Banana Bread

1½	cups sugar
½	cup shortening
2	eggs, beaten
1	tsp. vanilla
¼	cup dairy free milk (rice, almond, coconut or soy)
1	tsp. vinegar
2	cups gluten free all purpose flour
1	tsp. xanthan gum (if not in flour)
½	cup raisins (optional)
1	tsp. baking powder
½	tsp. baking soda
½	tsp. salt
1	cup bananas, (2 medium) mashed
½ -1	cup nuts, chopped (optional)

Preheat oven to 350°.

Mix all the ingredients until smooth. Pour into a greased loaf pan floured with gluten free flour. Bake 60-70 minutes. Makes 1 loaf.

- **Buy yeast in bulk. Split with a friend or freeze the extra that you don't use. Buying in bulk uses less packaging, which is less expensive and better for the environment.**

   Yeast is approximately $4.00 a pound in bulk compared to $35.00 a pound buying the little packets. If you don't have someone to split it with, buy bulk anyway. Even if half is wasted, it is still less expensive than the small packets. Extra yeast may be frozen for longer storage.

Pumpkin Bread

1½ cups sugar
2 eggs, slightly beaten
½ cup oil
1 cup pumpkin
1¾ cups gluten free all purpose flour
1 tsp. xanthan gum (if not in flour)
1 tsp. baking soda
¼ tsp. baking powder
1 tsp. salt
½ tsp. cinnamon
½ tsp. cloves
½ tsp. nutmeg
¼ tsp. allspice
⅓ cup water
½ cup raisins (optional)
½ cup nuts (optional)

Preheat oven to 350°.

Mix sugar, eggs, oil, and pumpkin in a bowl. Add dry ingredients and water in the order given. Mix well. Stir in nuts and raisins, if desired.

Pour into a greased loaf pan floured with gluten free flour and bake 1 hour (or longer, if needed). Makes 1 loaf.

To test if it is done, put a knife in the center of the bread. If it comes out clean, it is finished.

Serve with honey butter (p.342).

- **Spread dairy free butter on leftover hamburger and hot dog buns. Broil. Serve with jelly for a different toast. You could also spread with garlic butter and/or dairy free Parmesan cheese and broil.**

Notes

Soups And Sandwiches

Soup And Sandwich Tips

- **When making sandwiches,** use only one slice of lunch meat or, for items like tuna, spread thin on the bread.

- **Use vegetable scraps to make vegetable stock.** Save onion peels, carrot peels and celery tops. Tie in a cheese cloth and use to make vegetable, chicken or beef stock.

- **Use soy granules** for more protein in soups and casseroles.

- **Fry 1 pound of bacon.** When cool, crumble into pieces and freeze. When you need a little for flavor, simply take out a tablespoon or two.

- **When a recipe calls for parsley,** use the leaves from celery instead. Dry celery leaves and use in place of parsley flakes.

- **If you accidentally over-salt a dish:** While it's still cooking, drop in a peeled potato. It absorbs the excess salt for an instant fix.

- **Cut sandwiches into quarters** to make them "fancy". Even bologna sandwiches look tasty when cut like this.

- **Most soups only need ½ to 1 cup meat** even for a large pot of soup. Don't use more even if the recipe calls for it.

- **Adjust vegetables in your soup** to what you have on hand or what is on sale.

- **Stretch soup** with potatoes, gluten free pasta, or rice.

- **Don't throw out leftover or soggy salad.** Grind it up and add to vegetable soups.

- **Freeze broth in ice cube trays.** Each cube equals about ¼ cup. Easy measuring when you need just a little broth.

- **Instant mashed potatoes** make a great thickener for soups and stews.

Basic Soup Seasoning

4   Tbsp. basil
6   Tbsp. seasoned salt (p.320)
2   Tbsp. thyme
2   Tbsp. onion salt
2   Tbsp. garlic powder
2   Tbsp. sage
2   Tbsp. pepper
2   Tbsp. celery salt

Mix well. Store in an airtight container. Use 2-2½ teaspoons seasoning mix for each pot of soup.

Tomato Soup

2   Tbsp. cornstarch
1   Tbsp. sugar
2   cups dairy free milk (rice or soy), divided
1   Tbsp. dairy free butter
4   cups tomato juice, heated
    parsley, chopped

In a large saucepan, combine cornstarch, sugar and ¼ cup milk. Stir until smooth. Add remaining milk and butter.

Bring to a boil over medium heat, stirring constantly. Cook and stir for 2 minutes or until thickened.

Slowly stir in hot tomato juice until blended. Sprinkle with parsley. Serves 10-12.

Broccoli Soup

2½	cups broccoli, frozen*
¼	cup onion, chopped or 1 tsp. onion powder
2	cups chicken broth
1	Tbsp. cornstarch
½	tsp. garlic powder
1½	tsp. salt
	dash pepper
2	cups dairy free milk (rice or soy)
¼-½	lb. dairy free cheese

In a saucepan, combine broccoli, onion, and chicken broth. Bring to a boil. Simmer for 10 minutes or until broccoli is tender. Mix cornstarch with 2 Tbsp. cold water. Add cornstarch, garlic powder, onion powder (if using instead of onion), salt and pepper. Slowly stir in milk and add cheese. Cook, stirring constantly until cheese is melted. Do not boil.

*2½ cups fresh broccoli stems or flowers, cut into bite-size pieces may be used instead. This is a great way to use broccoli stems so they don't go to waste. Serves 6-8.

Broccoli Rice Soup

Add 2 cups of cooked rice to the broccoli soup.

Turkey Soup

turkey bones
water
salt (to taste)
garlic salt (to taste)
onion salt (to taste)
pepper (to taste)

Simmer turkey bones and water in a large pot, following directions for Basic Chicken Soup (below). Season with salts and pepper, to taste.

Basic Chicken Soup

2-3 chicken necks
2-4 chicken wings
3   qts. water
4   chicken bouillon cubes
1   tsp. salt
1   bay leaf
2   medium carrots, sliced
2   medium onions, diced
2   stalks celery, chopped

Bring first 6 ingredients just to boil in a large pot. Skim off foam and discard. Reduce heat and simmer, uncovered, 2½ hours or until the chicken is very tender.

Strain the liquid. Cool and refrigerate so the fat can be removed easily. Let the meat cool until it can be handled. Remove meat from bones. Discard bones. Skim fat. Bring to a boil and add the last 3 ingredients. Simmer 30 minutes and serve.

Makes about 12 cups broth or soup. Half the broth may be removed before adding vegetables and frozen up to 6 months. Makes 12 cups.

Mom's Stew

½   lb. round steak, cubed
6   cups water
1   bay leaf
1   tsp. salt
1   tsp. sugar
1   tsp. garlic salt, (or to taste)
1   tsp. onion salt, (or to taste) or 1 onion, chopped
¼   tsp. allspice
1   tsp. Worcestershire sauce
1   tsp. lemon juice
2   carrots, peeled and sliced
6   potatoes, peeled and diced
1   Tbsp. cornstarch
2   Tbsp. water

Brown meat in a large saucepan. Add all the other ingredients except vegetables, cornstarch and 2 tablespoons water and simmer for 1-2 hours, until meat is tender.

Add the vegetables and cook for 15-20 minutes, until tender.

Mix cornstarch and 2 tablespoons water. Add to boiling stew and simmer for 15 minutes, until thickened. Makes 2 quarts.

Great with cornbread (p.86) or Dinner Rolls (p.85).

- **If a recipe calls for herbs that don't dissolve, such as whole cloves, bay leaves and garlic cloves, tuck them into a metal tea ball and hook the chain over the side of the pot. This way it's easy to remove seasonings after cooking or before cooking is finished if the flavor is strong enough.**

Potato Soup

6   medium potatoes, peeled and cubed
     water
2   chicken bouillon cubes
2   slices bacon, fried and crumbled or 1 Tbsp. bacon grease
     pepper (to taste)
     salt (to taste)
2   cups dairy free American cheese
1   tsp. onion salt
4   cups dairy free milk (rice or soy)

In a Dutch oven, add potatoes and enough water to cover. Boil until potatoes are tender. Drain and add the rest of the ingredients. Cook just until heated through. Do not boil.

Elephant Soup

1   Elephant
     salt and pepper
2   rabbits (optional)

Cut the elephant into bite-size pieces. This will take about 3 months. Salt and pepper to taste. Cook over a kerosene fire at 470° for about 8 days. This will serve 3,800 people. If more are expected, add 2 rabbits. Do this only if necessary since most people do not like to find hare in their stew.

French Onion Soup

4   Tbsp. dairy free butter
4   onions, thinly sliced (yellow works best)
1   qt. beef stock or broth
1   bay leaf
4   slices toasted gluten free bread
1   cup dairy free mozzarella, grated

Melt butter in a skillet. Sauté onions until slightly brown. Add onions to beef stock and bay leaf in saucepan. Simmer slowly for 10 minutes.

Pour into four oven safe bowls. Place bread on top of each bowl of soup. Sprinkle the cheese on top. Then set under broiler and cook until cheese is melted and brown. Serves 4.

This soup can simmer in the crockpot on low overnight.

Bacon Bean Soup

8   slices bacon, diced
½   onion, chopped
2   cloves garlic, crushed
2   (16 oz.) cans ranch style beans
½   cup cooked rice
1   (8 oz.) can stewed tomatoes
2   tsp. salt
     dash of pepper and paprika
4   cups water

Fry diced bacon in a saucepan. Drain. Sauté onions and garlic in bacon fat until the onions are golden. Add remaining ingredients and simmer 1½ hours to allow flavors to blend. Add water as needed during cooking. Serves 4.

Chili

½ lb. ground beef
1   onion, chopped
1   green pepper, chopped
1   (8 oz.) can tomato sauce
1   (28 oz.) can tomatoes (Do not drain.)
1   tsp. salt
⅛ tsp. paprika
⅛ tsp. cayenne pepper
1-3 Tbsp. chili powder (to taste)
1   tsp. garlic powder
1   (15 oz.) can kidney beans (drained) or
      2 cups cooked kidney beans (optional)

Cook and stir ground beef, onion and green pepper in a large 10-inch skillet until beef is brown and the onion is tender. Drain.

Stir in tomato sauce, tomatoes (with liquid), salt, paprika, cayenne pepper, chili powder and garlic powder. Heat to boiling. Reduce heat. Simmer, uncovered, for 30 minutes.

If using beans, add beans to chili. One can of tomato juice may be added to make more chili. Serves 4.

• **Grease the inside of the crockpot for easy cleanup.**

• **Ketchup, can be bought in large containers. Freeze in 2½ cup portions, which is the amount that will fill an empty standard bottle.**

Vegetable Soup

1   beef soup bone
2   qts. water
2   bay leaves
2   Tbsp. salt
      pepper (to taste)
2   (16 oz.) cans whole peeled tomatoes
4   medium potatoes, pared and chopped
3   stalks celery, sliced
1   large onion, chopped
3   large carrots, peeled and sliced
2   cups rice or GF pasta, cooked

Place soup bone in a large Dutch oven and cover with water. Add bay leaves. Simmer 2 hours. Remove the soup bone. Let stock cool. Skim fat. Add remaining ingredients, except rice or pasta, and simmer 2 more hours. Add rice 5 minutes before serving. Remove bay leaf. Adjust seasoning. This soup is best if eaten the next day. Makes 3 quarts.

Husbands are the best people to tell secrets to.

They will never tell anyone

because they aren't listening to you.

Egg Drop Soup

1   green onion, chopped (top included)
2   eggs, slightly beaten
3   cups chicken broth
¼   tsp. salt
      dash pepper

Stir onion into eggs. Heat broth to boiling in a 3-quart saucepan. Add salt and pepper. Pour egg mixture slowly into broth, stirring constantly with a fork. Boil about 5 minutes until eggs are done. Serves 4-6.

Onion Soup Mix

¾   cup instant minced onion
4   tsp. onion powder
⅓   cup beef bouillon powder
¼   tsp. celery seeds, crushed
¼   tsp. sugar

Mix all ingredients and store in an airtight container.

To use: Add 2 tablespoons mix to 1 cup boiling water. Cover and simmer 15 minutes.

This makes a stronger soup than the store bought mix, so you can use less.

Fried Egg Sandwich

1 egg
1 tsp. dairy free butter
2 slices gluten free bread

Heat dairy free butter in a large skillet. Crack egg into a cup and beat slightly. Pour into hot skillet and let cook 3 to 5 minutes until it sets. Carefully turn egg over with a spatula and fry on the other side. Serve between 2 pieces of bread. Makes 1 sandwich.

Sloppy Joes

1 lb. ground beef
1 medium onion, chopped, or ½ tsp. onion powder
½ tsp. garlic powder
5 Tbsp. ketchup
2 tsp. brown sugar
⅛ tsp. lemon juice
1 Tbsp. Worcestershire sauce
½ tsp. salt
6 gluten free hamburger buns

Brown meat and onion until onion is tender. Drain fat. Add other ingredients and heat thoroughly. Serve on hamburger buns.
Serves 6.

- **Spread leftover sloppy Joe meat in a casserole dish. Place sliced dairy free American cheese over the meat and top the cheese with gluten free biscuits (p.92). Bake at 350° until the biscuits are done.**

Chicken Salad

1½   cups chicken or turkey, cooked and chopped
½   cup mayonnaise or dairy free salad dressing
1   small stalk celery, chopped
1   small onion, chopped, or 1 tsp. onion powder
¼   tsp. salt
¼   tsp. pepper

Mix all ingredients. Best if chilled for 1 or 2 hours. Serve on lettuce or gluten free bread.

Ham Salad

Substitute ham for chicken or turkey. Omit salt and pepper and add 1 teaspoon prepared mustard.

Egg Salad

Substitute 6 hard-boiled eggs, chopped, for the chicken.

Tuna Salad

Substitute 1 can tuna, drained, for the chicken.

- **To help keep eggs from cracking while boiling, add vinegar to the water.**

Hot Roast Beef Sandwich

1-2 cups leftover roast beef (p.184)
2   cups leftover roast gravy (p.184)
4   pieces gluten free bread

Warm roast and gravy. Pour over bread or toast. Serve warm.
Serves 4.

French Dip

1   roast, slow cooked and sliced thin
      juice from roast, or make your own with beef bouillon cubes
      toasted gluten free bread

Layer thin pieces of roast on toasted bread. Warm juice in bowls
and serve for dipping sandwiches. Juice may be extended by adding
some water and bouillon to suit your taste. An onion could be added
to the roast while cooking; place a slice or two on the sandwich.

An optimist is a person who expects the

ketchup to come out in 3 shakes.

Hamburger Gravy On Toast

½   lb. ground beef, browned
    white gravy (p.178)
    toasted gluten free bread

Make white gravy from hamburger drippings and add hamburger. Cook until warmed through. Serve on toast. Serves 4.

Easy Pizza

gluten free bread, toasted
pizza sauce (p.210)
dairy free mozzarella cheese

Toppings of your choice:

olives
mushrooms
peppers
hamburger
sausage
onions

Preheat oven to 350°. Top bread with sauce, then cheese and then toppings. Bake until thoroughly warmed and cheese begins to bubble and brown, about 15 minutes. Serves 4.

Vegetables

Vegetable And Bean Tips

- **To make peeling vegetables and fruits like tomatoes and peaches easier,** carve an x on the bottom of them and place in the microwave. Microwave on high for 35-45 seconds. Remove from microwave and peel.

- **Peel broccoli stems.** It makes them very tender. You could use them for soup or in any dish calling for broccoli.

- **If potatoes get eyes,** cut them into halves or fourths (as long as they have about 3-4 eyes on each chunk) and plant them in the garden or flower bed. In a couple months, you can dig them up and have new potatoes.

- **Keep a container in the freezer** for the leftover water from steaming vegetables. Then, when you have enough, use it as vegetable broth.

- **Save bacon grease for flavoring** your dishes instead of butter or margarine.

- **Save your frying oil** in the refrigerator and use again later.

- **To store onions:** Put one onion in a pantyhose leg and tie a knot. Then put another onion and tie another knot until the pantyhose leg is full. To remove an onion, cut at the top of the next knot.

- **Wrap celery in aluminum foil** when putting it in the refrigerator. It will keep for weeks.

- **Use beans instead of meat in dishes.**

- **Renew limp celery** by soaking in ice water.

- **When boiling corn on the cob,** add a pinch of sugar to help bring out the corn's natural sweetness.

- **When you have leftover tomatoes or other veggies**, make a puree of them and freeze in ice cube trays. After they are frozen, put them in a plastic bag. The next time you make soup or stew or need them for seasoning something, use only as many cubes as you need.

Baked Beans

1   (16 oz.) can of pork and beans
1   tsp. mustard
1   Tbsp. bacon grease
4   Tbsp. brown sugar
2   Tbsp. onion, chopped or ½ tsp. onion powder

Put all the ingredients in a saucepan and mix thoroughly. Let simmer on medium heat 15-30 minutes. These can simmer longer if needed. Serve warm. You can also bake these in the oven for 1 hour at 250° until thickened. Serves 4.

Green Beans

1   pound green beans or 1 (16 oz.) can green beans
4   slices bacon*
1-2 Tbsp. onion chopped
1   tsp. salt
¼   tsp. pepper

Snip off the ends of the green beans and slice into thin slivers. (If using canned beans, open the can and drain.)

Fry bacon until crisp. Remove bacon from pan and drain on paper towels. Cool and break into pieces. Remove all but 2 tablespoons bacon grease.

Chop onion and sauté until limp. Add beans, stir thoroughly and cook over moderate heat for about 1 minute. Add 1 tablespoon water. Cover and cook 4 additional minutes.

Remove cover. Continue to cook and stir until beans are tender, but still crisp. Season with salt and pepper and add bacon bits. Serves 4.

*You may substitute 2 tablespoons bacon grease for the bacon.

Herbed Broccoli

1   lb. broccoli
2   Tbsp. vegetable oil
1   tsp. fresh oregano, chopped or ¼ tsp. dried oregano
½   tsp. salt
1   tsp. fresh basil, chopped or ¼ tsp. dried basil
1   clove garlic, crushed
2   plum tomatoes, chopped

Steam broccoli until done. Heat oil in a 10-inch skillet on medium heat. Add all ingredients except the broccoli. Heat about 1 minute, stirring frequently, until hot. Pour over broccoli and mix gently. Serves 4.

Glazed Carrots

½   lb. fresh carrots or baby carrots
4   Tbsp. dairy free butter
6   Tbsp. brown sugar
1   tsp. cinnamon
1   tsp. ginger (optional)

Clean carrots and cut into bite-size pieces. Steam 10 minutes in a small amount of boiling water just until tender.

Melt dairy free butter in a large skillet over low heat. Add brown sugar, cinnamon, and ginger. Cook 1-2 minutes.

Add hot carrots, stirring well to coat. Remove when shiny and well glazed. Serves 4.

Creamy Carrot Casserole

4   cups carrots, sliced
¾   cup dairy free salad dressing (Miracle Whip)
¼   cup onion, chopped
¼   tsp. salt
¼   tsp. pepper
14   gluten free crackers, crushed
1   Tbsp. dairy free butter, melted
2   Tbsp. parsley
½   cup shredded dairy free cheese

Put carrots in 1½ quart microwave safe casserole with 2 tablespoons water. Cover and cook in the microwave on high 6-8 minutes or until tender. Stir once. Drain.

Mix salad dressing, onion, salt, and pepper. Add carrots. Toss crackers, butter, and parsley. Spoon over carrots. Cook in microwave uncovered 3 minutes. Add cheese. Cook 1-2 minutes longer until cheese is melted. Serves 4.

Flavored Vegetable Butters

Mix one of the following in ¼ cup softened dairy free butter, to flavor your plain vegetables.

- 1 tsp. basil, fresh, chopped or ½ tsp. dried

- 1 Tbsp. chives, chopped and 1 Tbsp. parsley, chopped

- ½ clove garlic, crushed, or ½ tsp. garlic powder

- 1 Tbsp. prepared horseradish

- 1 Tbsp. lemon peel, grated, and 2 Tbsp. lemon juice

- ¼ tsp. dry mustard and 1 tsp. fresh dill or ¼ tsp. dried dill

Cheesy Cauliflower

1   medium head cauliflower

Topping

½   cup mayonnaise
½   tsp. onion salt or 1 tsp. onion, finely chopped
1   tsp. mustard
½   cup dairy free Cheddar cheese

Wash cauliflower, don't dry. Place cauliflower in a casserole dish. Cover with plastic wrap. Microwave 8-9 minutes until tender.

Combine mayonnaise, onion salt or onion and mustard. Spoon on cauliflower and sprinkle cheese on top. Microwave 1-2 minutes to melt cheese. Serves 4.

Cucumbers And Tomatoes

2   medium cucumbers
2   Tbsp. dairy free butter
1   onion, sliced and separated into rings
2   medium tomatoes, cut into wedges
½   tsp. salt
     dash of pepper
1   Tbsp. fresh dill, chopped or 1 tsp. dried dill

Wash and remove seeds from cucumbers. Slice into 1 inch pieces. Heat dairy free butter in a 12-inch skillet over medium heat. Cook cucumbers and onion in butter about 5 minutes, stirring occasionally (just until cucumbers are tender).

Stir in tomatoes. Sprinkle with salt and pepper. Cook just until tomatoes are hot. Sprinkle with dill. Serves 4.

Grilled Corn

4   ears corn
2   Tbsp. dairy free butter
1   Tbsp. taco seasoning (p.320) or lemon pepper
2   Tbsp. water

Husk and clean corn. Mix dairy free butter and taco seasoning. Spread over corn. Place each ear on a double thickness of aluminum foil. Sprinkle corn with water. Wrap securely in aluminum foil and twist the ends tight. Place on medium coals and grill 15-35 minutes (until tender), turning once. Serves 4.

Egg Rolls

½   lb. beef, pork or chicken, cooked and diced small
2   cups cabbage, chopped
½   cup carrots, shredded
3   green onions or ¼ cup onion, chopped or 1 tsp. onion powder
½   tsp. ginger
½   tsp. salt
2   Tbsp. gluten free soy sauce
1   pkg. rice wrappers
      vegetable oil
      mustard, ketchup, or sweet and sour sauce (p.335)

Add 1 tablespoon oil in a frying pan. Heat pan very hot and add meat. Cook 1-2 minutes, until lightly browned. Add cabbage, carrots and onions and cook 2 minutes. Stir in ginger, salt and soy sauce. Let cool 5 minutes.

Follow the directions on the back of the rice wrappers for wrapping. Use 2 tablespoons filling for each egg roll. Deep fry 2-4 egg rolls at a time at 350° for 2-3 minutes, turning occasionally. Drain on paper towels. Serve warm with choice of sauces. Makes 20 egg rolls.

Rice wrappers can usually be found in the produce department.

Baked Onions

2-4 onions

Preheat oven to 350°. Place unpeeled onions in a pan to catch the juice. Bake about 30 minutes. Time and temperature can be adjusted if you are baking other things. Peel before eating. Baking makes the onions very sweet. Serves 2-4.

Baked Onion Slices

4   large onions, peeled and sliced
¼   cup vinegar
¼   cup sugar
¼   cup dairy free butter, melted
¼   cup boiling water

Preheat oven to 300°. Arrange onions in a casserole. Combine other ingredients. Pour over onions and bake 1 hour. Serves 4.

Barbecued Onions

6   medium onions
6   bouillon cubes (any flavor)
3   Tbsp. dairy free butter
       pepper (to taste)

Peel onions. Scoop out a hole in the top of each onion. Fill each with a bouillon cube, ½ teaspoon butter and pepper. Wrap onions separately in foil. Place on barbecue grill, turning frequently, for 30 minutes. Serves 6.

- **To remove onion smell from your hands: Rub a stainless steel spoon between your hands under running water.**

Baked Potato Toppings

- chili with dairy free Cheddar cheese

- dairy free sour cream and chives

- onion, bacon, dairy free sour cream, and chives

- broccoli and dairy free cheese (Melt the cheese on top in the oven.)

- pizza (pizza sauce, dairy free cheese, pepperoni, sausage, olives, mushrooms)

- taco salad (hamburger with taco seasoning, lettuce, tomatoes, onions, grated dairy free cheese, dairy free sour cream, salsa, canned peppers)

- peppers, onions

- bacon bits

- ranch dressing

French Fries

potatoes, peeled or unpeeled
vegetable oil for frying
salt (to taste)

Use 1 potato per person. If using unpeeled potatoes, wash thoroughly. Dry. Slice potato into ¼ inch thick strips. If you are unable to use right away, store in salted water. Dry well with a paper towel.

Pour vegetable oil into a deep saucepan and heat to 375°. Fry potato fries in vegetable oil until golden brown. Remove with a slotted spoon and drain on paper towels. Fry again for 3-5 minutes for extra crispy French fries.

Fried Potatoes

6   potatoes, peeled and sliced
2-3 Tbsp. bacon grease or dairy free butter
    salt and pepper
    garlic cloves (as desired)
    parsley (as desired)

Melt bacon grease or dairy free butter in a frying pan. Add the potatoes in the pan and cook over medium heat. When brown, flip potatoes and cook until tender. Remove from pan. Salt and pepper to taste. Serves 4-6.

Lemon Potatoes

10 new potatoes or 5 medium potatoes, cut into halves or quarters
2   Tbsp. dairy free butter
½   tsp. lemon peel, grated
1   Tbsp. lemon juice
2   tsp. chives, chopped
½   tsp. salt
⅛   tsp. pepper
    dash of nutmeg

Clean and steam potatoes 20 minutes (until tender). Heat the remaining ingredients just to boiling to make lemon butter. Pour the lemon butter over the potatoes and serve. Serves 5-6.

- **To keep potatoes from budding, place an apple in the bag with the potatoes.**

Mashed Potatoes

5   large potatoes, peeled and cubed
2   Tbsp. sugar
2   Tbsp. mayonnaise
2   Tbsp. dairy free butter
1   tsp. salt
½   cup chicken broth

In a large saucepan, place potatoes and enough water to cover the potatoes. Bring to a boil. Reduce heat. Cover and simmer until potatoes are tender (about 10-15 minutes depending on your altitude). Drain. Transfer potatoes to a mixing bowl and mash. I use a hand mixer for this but you can use a potato masher. Add mayonnaise, dairy free butter, chicken broth, sugar and salt. Beat until smooth. Serves 5-6.

Garlic Mashed Potatoes

Add 15 cloves garlic, peeled and halved, to the potatoes when boiling.

Oven Fried Potatoes

4   potatoes, thinly sliced
4   Tbsp. vegetable oil
    garlic powder

Preheat oven to 325°. Rub each potato slice with oil. Spread out on a cookie sheet and sprinkle with garlic powder. Bake 30 minutes. Serves 4.

- **If homemade mashed potatoes are too moist, add a few instant potato flakes until they are the right consistency.**

Cheesy Potatoes

1   potato per person, peeled and sliced
     dairy free butter
     dairy free cheese

Place potatoes in a microwave or oven safe casserole dish. Put
1 teaspoon butter per potato dotted over the top. Microwave 5-7
minutes or bake in the oven 20 minutes or until potatoes are tender.

Add as much shredded cheese as desired and microwave 1-2 more
minutes or place back in the oven until the cheese is melted.

Potato Pancakes

2   cups leftover mashed potatoes
2   Tbsp. gluten free all purpose flour
1   egg
     dairy free butter

Mix first 3 ingredients. Make into patties and fry in dairy free butter
until golden brown on each side. Serve warm with dairy free butter.
Delicious served with applesauce. Serves 2.

Potato Peels

     potatoes
     salt
     pepper
     garlic powder
     onion powder
     dairy free Cheddar cheese, shredded

Grease a cookie sheet and preheat oven to 400°. Wash and peel
potatoes with a knife (trying to get large pieces). Put peels in a bowl
and add the spices to taste. Mix well. Bake 8-10 minutes until crisp.

Remove from oven and sprinkle cheese on the potato skins. Return to
the oven for 2 or 3 minutes until the cheese melts.

Scalloped Potatoes

⅓ cup gluten free all purpose flour
1 tsp. onion powder (optional)
   salt and pepper (to taste)
3 cups chicken broth
4 cups potatoes, sliced
1 onion, sliced
   ham, bacon or sausage, diced (optional)
3 Tbsp. dairy free butter

Preheat oven to 325°. Place the flour, onion powder (if using instead of onion) and salt and pepper into a quart jar. Close and shake thoroughly. Add broth. Close and shake again until all the flour is dissolved.

In a greased 3 quart casserole dish, layer the potatoes, onions, and meat (if using it), dotting each layer with butter. Add the flour-milk mixture. Bake 1½ hours. Serves 4.

Au Gratin Potatoes

Add 1½ cups of cubed or shredded dairy free cheese.

- **Buy ½ pound of garlic. Chop in the food processor. Place in a heavy duty freezer bag and lay flat on a tray. Freeze. The garlic will break into small pieces to be used as needed.**

- **Potatoes should be stored in a cool, dry, dark place, but not refrigerated.**

Sweet Potato Casserole

3   cups sweet potatoes, mashed
½   cup dairy free butter, melted
½   cup sugar
2   eggs
1   Tbsp. vanilla

Topping

1   cup brown sugar, packed
1   cup pecans
½   cup gluten free all purpose flour
⅓   cup dairy free butter, melted

Preheat oven to 350°. Mix all the ingredients and put into a 9x9 inch casserole dish buttered with dairy free butter. Mix topping ingredients and sprinkle over the top. Bake uncovered for 20 minutes.

This is a great dish for holiday dinners and potlucks as it can be made up the day before and then baked the next day. Serves 8-9.

Sweet Potato Chips

2   medium sweet potatoes
2   Tbsp. olive oil
    salt and pepper
    paprika

Preheat oven to 450°. Peel sweet potatoes and slice as thinly as possible. Toss with 2 tablespoons of olive oil and spread in a thin layer on a cookie sheet. Sprinkle with salt, pepper and paprika.

Bake about 20 minutes or until crispy. Makes 4 servings.

Mexican Summer Squash

4   yellow summer squash
4   ears of corn
3   ripe tomatoes
¼   cup dairy free butter
1   small onion, chopped
     salt and pepper (to taste)

Wash squash and cut into small pieces. Cut the corn from the cob. Peel tomatoes and cut into cubes. (The skin comes off the tomatoes easily if you dip in boiling water for 1 minute before peeling.)

Heat butter in a saucepan. Stir in onion and cook until limp but not brown. Add squash, corn, tomatoes, salt and pepper. Cover and cook over low heat for 30-40 minutes, stirring occasionally. If desired serve over cooked rice. Serves 4.

Baked Squash

2   squash (any kind of yellow squash)
4   slices of bacon or 2 Tbsp. bacon grease
     salt and pepper (to taste)
     brown sugar

Preheat oven to 350°. Wash squash and cut them in half. Spoon out the seeds and fibers from the center. Put 4 slices of bacon in a shallow baking pan and bake until crisp. If using bacon grease, just heat in the oven until bacon grease is melted.

Remove bacon and drain on paper towels. Sprinkle squash with salt and pepper. Then place cut side down in bacon grease.

Bake at 350° for 1 hour or until tender. Just before serving, brush the inside with some bacon grease, sprinkle lightly with brown sugar, and sprinkle the crumbled bacon into the squash cavity. Serves 4.

Fried Mushrooms, Zucchini, Onion Rings, Green Tomatoes And Squash

	mushrooms
	zucchini
	onions
	squash
	green tomatoes
	gluten free all purpose flour
1	egg, beaten
½	cup dairy free milk (rice or soy)
	gluten free cracker crumbs
	vegetable oil for frying
	salt and pepper

Wash all of the vegetables. Slice the zucchini, onions, squash and green tomatoes into thin slices. Put some gluten free all purpose flour into a bowl. Put the egg and milk into another bowl and mix. Place cracker crumbs into a bowl.

Pour the vegetable oil into a deep saucepan or frying pan and heat to 375° or until a few cracker crumbs fry quickly.

Dip the vegetables into flour, then the egg mixture, then cracker crumbs and fry until golden. Drain on paper towels. Salt and pepper to taste. Serve hot with dairy free ranch dressing.

Tact is the ability to close your mouth

before someone else wants you to.

Scalloped Tomatoes

6   ripe tomatoes or 1 (20 oz.) can tomatoes
1   cup coarse dry gluten free bread crumbs
1   tsp. sugar
     salt and pepper (to taste)
3-6 Tbsp. dairy free butter

Preheat oven to 350°. Skin tomatoes and cut into slices. The skins will slide right off if you dip them in boiling water for 1 minute first.

Combine bread crumbs, sugar, salt, pepper and butter. Add more butter if you want the mixture less dry.

Place a layer of tomatoes in the bottom of a casserole dish buttered with dairy free butter and sprinkle with some of the bread crumb mixture. Repeat layers of tomato and crumb mixture until the dish is filled and top with the remaining crumb mixture. Bake 30 minutes. Serves 6.

Southern Scalloped Tomatoes

Increase sugar to ¾ cup and then mix all the other ingredients together. Bring to a boil in a heavy skillet and add tomatoes. Cook slowly for 1 hour until tomatoes are glazed. If they start to look dry, add more butter.

• **Canned beans and other canned ingredients sometimes stick to the bottom of the can and require a spatula to remove. Try opening the bottom of the can instead. Shake and everything should fall out easily.**

• **Chop tomatoes in the can. Insert a knife and cut against the sides of can. Why wash a cutting board when you don't have to?**

Stewed Tomatoes

3   large tomatoes, ripe or 1 (28 oz.) can peeled tomatoes
1   medium onion, finely chopped
2   Tbsp. green bell pepper, finely chopped
½   tsp. salt
⅛   tsp. pepper
1   Tbsp. sugar
2   slices gluten free bread, toasted and cut into ½ inch cubes

Dip tomatoes into boiling water for 1 minute. Peel. The skin should slip off easily. Cut the tomatoes into small pieces. Mix all ingredients except bread in a 2½ quart saucepan. Cover and heat to boiling. Reduce heat. Simmer about 10 minutes (until the tomatoes are soft). Stir in bread cubes. Serve warm. Serves 4.

Egg Noodles

2   eggs
½   tsp. salt
¼   cup dairy free milk (rice or soy)
2-3   cups gluten free all purpose flour

Beat eggs slightly. Add salt and milk. Mix in 2 cups flour. Thoroughly mix with your hands. Add enough additional flour to make a stiff dough. Turn dough onto a counter or board that has been well floured with gluten free flour. Knead until smooth and elastic. Cover. Let rest 10 minutes.

Roll dough very thin. Cut dough into ⅛ inch strips to desired length. Let dry 2-3 hours*, turning once. When ready to use, drop into boiling water or broth. Boil 12 to 15 minutes. Drain thoroughly if cooking in water.

*Noodles may dry longer if you need to make them in the morning for dinner.

Cooked Dry Beans

2   cups beans
5   cups water
     ham bone (optional)
1   onion (optional)
2   tsp. salt

Wash and drain beans. Put beans, water, ham bone, and onion, if desired, into a large pan and bring to a boil. Boil 2 minutes. Remove from heat. Cover and let stand 1 hour.

Add salt. Cover and boil gently 1½-2 hours or until tender. Add more water during cooking if needed. Makes 5 cups cooked beans.

Dry Beans Quick Prep Tips

Soak any kind of dry beans overnight. Drain. Freeze beans in 2 to 4 cup portions.

To prepare: Cook beans in boiling water for 20 minutes. They will soften very easily if they are frozen first.

To help with unpleasant bean side effects, you can rinse the beans after soaking and add ½ teaspoon baking soda when cooking the dry beans.

Refried Beans

1   (20 oz.) can kidney or pinto beans or
       2½ cups cooked kidney or pinto beans
1-2 Tbsp. bacon grease or vegetable oil
1   small onion, grated
1   clove garlic, finely chopped
½   green pepper, finely chopped
1   tsp. chili powder
½   tsp. cumin
4-5 Tbsp. hot beef broth
      salt (to taste)

Drain beans, reserving the liquid. Mash beans thoroughly. Heat grease in a skillet. Add onion, garlic, and green pepper. Cook over low heat until tender.

Stir in chili powder, cumin and hot beef broth. Then add the beans. Cook slowly, stirring continuously. Add bean liquid as needed.

The beans are cooked when they are completely dry. Salt as desired. Makes 3 cups.

I dusted. It came back.

I am not falling for that again.

White Sauce
Dairy Free Cream Soup

1   cup dairy free milk (rice and soy)
2   Tbsp. cornstarch
     dash salt
1   Tbsp. dairy free butter

In a bowl, combine milk, cornstarch and salt. Mix well. Mix until all the ingredients are dissolved.

Melt butter in a 1 quart saucepan. Stir in cornstarch-milk mixture and cook over low heat until mixture thickens and starts to bubble. Keep stirring until thickened completely.

This recipe equals 1 can of cream soup. It can be doubled, but add only 1¾ cups water. Makes 1 cup. May be doubled or tripled easily to fit your needs.

Chicken Sauce

Substitute cold chicken stock in place of the milk. Omit the salt.

Cheese Sauce

Add ½ cup dairy free shredded Cheddar cheese to the white sauce. Heat over low heat, stirring until all the cheese is melted.

- **To avoid wasting dairy free sour cream, serve with a knife rather than a spoon. You can easily scrape the knife off on the edge of the container or serving dish, reducing waste and using every last bit.**

Broccoli And Pasta

1   medium head fresh broccoli
3   Tbsp. dairy free butter
¼   cup olive oil or vegetable oil
1   medium onion, chopped
4   cloves garlic, minced
½   cup chicken broth
      salt and pepper (to taste)
1   (12 oz.) pkg. gluten free pasta, cooked
      dairy free Parmesan type cheese, grated

Wash and cut broccoli into bite-size pieces. Steam until just cooked. Drain well and set aside.

In a pan, melt butter and oil. Sauté onion until translucent. Add garlic and simmer for 1 minute. Add broccoli and broth. Simmer 3 minutes. Add salt and pepper.

In a large bowl, mix drained pasta with broccoli mixture. Toss well. Top with grated cheese and serve immediately. Serves 4.

Stewed Tomato Pasta

2   (14½ oz.) cans stewed tomatoes, with juice
1¾   cups chicken broth
2   Tbsp. vegetable oil
1   tsp. Italian seasoning
1   (12 oz.) pkg. spiral gluten free pasta

In a Dutch oven, combine everything but the pasta. Bring to a boil and add pasta. Reduce heat. Cover and simmer for 16-18 minutes, until pasta is tender. Stir occasionally. Serves 8-10.

Quick Pasta

½   lb. gluten free spaghetti
3   Tbsp. olive oil
1   cup salsa
1½ cups dairy free cheese, grated

Cook pasta and drain. Toss with the olive oil to coat. Add salsa and cheese. Toss again. Serves 2.

Restaurant Style Pasta Fagioli

1   (15 oz.) can great northern beans, undrained, or
      2 cups great northern beans, cooked
1   (28 oz.) can stewed tomatoes, sliced
16 oz. spaghetti sauce (p.210)
    Italian seasoning (to taste)
2   stalks celery, sliced thin
1   small onion, chopped
2   cups small gluten free spiral pasta, uncooked
    salt and pepper (to taste)

In a Dutch oven, combine everything and bring to a boil on medium high. Turn heat down to low. Cover pan with a lid and allow to cook on a slow simmer for 30 minutes or until pasta is tender. Stir occasionally. Serves 6.

- **Add one tablespoon of oil to the water for boiling pasta. This keeps the pasta from sticking.**

- **Add ¼ teaspoon garlic powder to pasta water when cooking for a wonderful flavor.**

Rice

Servings	1 cup	4 cups	6 cups
Water	1 cup	3 cups	4 cups
Salt	¼ tsp.	1 tsp.	1 tsp.
Rice	⅓ cup	1⅓ cups	2 cups

Use the given amounts of water, salt and rice to make the needed servings. To retain vitamins and minerals, do not rinse rice. Heat water and salt to boiling. Stir in rice. Cover tightly and cook slowly about 25 minutes, until rice is tender. Add a little water during cooking if rice becomes dry. Gently stir only if needed to keep rice from sticking.

Seasoned Rice Mix

1   cup gluten free spaghetti, broken into very small pieces
2   cups rice, uncooked
¼   cup dried parsley flakes
6   Tbsp. instant chicken or beef bouillon powder
2   tsp. onion powder
½   tsp. garlic powder
¼   tsp. dried thyme

Mix all the ingredients and store in an airtight container. To use, put 1 cup mix, 2 tablespoons dairy free butter, and 2 cups water into a saucepan. Bring to a boil. Cover, reduce heat and simmer 15 minutes or until the rice is tender. Makes 3 cups uncooked.

• **Use leftover rice for soups, casseroles, Spanish rice, fried rice, rice and beans, or on tortillas for burritos.**

Cheesy Rice
And Tomatoes

3   Tbsp. oil
1   medium onion, chopped
3   stalks celery, chopped
1   green pepper, chopped
2   cups cooked tomatoes or stewed tomatoes
3   cups cooked rice
2   cups dairy free cheese, shredded
1   tsp. salt
    dash pepper

In a pan with oil, sauté onion, celery and green pepper. Add tomatoes, rice, cheese, salt and pepper. Cover and simmer until cheese is melted. Serves 8.

Fried Rice

½   green pepper, finely chopped
1   tsp. dairy free butter
2   eggs
4   cups rice, cooked
2   Tbsp. gluten free soy sauce

Sauté green pepper in a skillet with butter. Add eggs and stir until scrambled and set. Add rice and soy sauce. Heat through. Serves 8.

Spanish Rice

1   chicken bouillon cube
½   cup water
1   cup rice, cooked
1   Tbsp. (or less) taco seasoning (p.320)
1   clove garlic, minced
1   cup tomato sauce (or 1 cup salsa)

Preheat oven to 375°. Dissolve bouillon in water. Mix all the ingredients and bake uncovered for 30 minutes. Serves 4.

Red Beans And Rice

1   cup white rice
1   small onion, chopped
2   (15 oz.) cans dark red kidney beans, or
       4 cups cooked kidney beans
2   (15 oz.) cans diced tomatoes
      garlic salt (to taste)
      oregano (to taste)
      basil (to taste)
      dairy free grated Cheddar cheese (optional)

Prepare rice. In a skillet with a cover, sauté the onion until translucent. Add remaining ingredients and cook over medium heat until bubbly, stirring occasionally. Cover, lower heat, and simmer about 15 minutes.

Serve over rice. Top with grated Cheddar cheese (if desired).
Serves 8.

- **Leftover beans? Add to Jambalaya, Spanish rice or red beans and rice instead of meat.**

- **Leftover rice? Sauté onion in dairy free butter. Add rice and chopped up leftover meat. Season with garlic powder, salt and pepper.**

Japanese Goulash

2   pieces bacon, fried and crumbled, or ½ cup ham, diced
       ½ cup hamburger, browned,
1   egg
2-3 cups cooked rice
1   carrot, finely diced

Fry meat in a skillet. Drain fat. Scramble egg. Add meat, rice and carrot to the skillet with the egg. Cook until warmed. Serve with gluten free soy sauce.

Stuffing Mix

6   cups cubed gluten free bread
1   Tbsp. parsley flakes
3   Tbsp. chicken bouillon powder
¼   cup dried minced onion
½   cup dried minced celery, or fresh celery may be sautéed
       and added just before cooking
1   tsp. thyme
1   tsp. pepper
½   tsp. sage
½   tsp. salt

Preheat oven 350°. Spread the bread cubes on a cookie sheet and bake 8 to 10 minutes, turning to brown evenly. Cool.

In a plastic bag or bowl, toss the bread cubes with the rest of the ingredients until well coated. Store in a tightly closed container in the pantry up to 4 months or in the freezer for up to a year.

To use: Combine 2 cups stuffing mix with ½ cup water and 2 tablespoons melted dairy free butter. Stir to combine thoroughly. Warm on the stovetop or in a microwave.

Stir again just before serving. Serves 8-12.

Homemade Stuffing

This is my Grandma Tatum's stuffing recipe (Jill's Mom). It is one of my favorite traditional Thanksgiving recipes! It has been in our family for years and is a family favorite! -Tawra

I hesitated to include our stuffing recipe because it is one of those recipes where it is hard to give exact measurements. You can adjust any of these ingredients to suit your taste and, if you want, you can add different things to the dish.

For example, you can replace some of the bread with cornbread or you can add mushrooms, celery, apples, giblets and many other things according to your own taste. This recipe may look complicated but it is really easy once you make it.

For a drier stuffing, use less liquid and for a more moist dressing, add more dairy free butter. Butter doesn't evaporate and won't make your dressing "soggy" the way liquid will. You can also add a little dairy free milk (rice or soy) if the stuffing seems too dry.

When you bake stuffing inside a turkey, or if you cook it in a covered pan, the stuffing won't dry out, so keep this in mind when testing how moist it is.

If you want your stuffing to be more fluffy, beat the eggs in the recipe before adding.

Homemade Stuffing
(Continued)

Here is the basic homemade stuffing recipe:

8-10	cups dried gluten free bread, cubed
½-1	lb. pork sausage
½-1	onion (or onion powder, to taste)
1½	cups broth*
¼-½	cup dairy free butter
1	chicken bouillon cube
3	eggs, slightly beaten
3	heaping tsp. ground sage
	salt and pepper

Place cubed bread in a very large mixing bowl. Let it sit out overnight if not dry enough.

Fry sausage and onion. I don't like celery in my dressing but if you do, you can add it at this time. Drain and add to the bowl of bread.

Pour the broth into a large measuring cup. Add butter and bouillon cube and heat in the microwave to melt. Pour this mixture and eggs over bread. Add sage, salt, pepper and onion powder (if not using onions).

Preheat oven to 350°. Using your hands, blend it all together until well mixed. Place in a well greased casserole dish or pan. Cover. Bake 30-45 minutes.

If you like your stuffing soft on the inside with a crispy crust, remove the cover for the last 15 minutes. If your dressing seems too dry, add a little dairy free milk for more moisture.

*For broth, I simmer the neck and giblets in a pan of water for an hour or two as soon as I take them out of the turkey. Then I use this water and some broth from the turkey, which has been cooking, to make my 1½ cups.

If you are baking your stuffing in the turkey and can't tell if it is done, just test with a meat thermometer and it should be 165°.

Notes

Salads

Salads, Dressings & Pickles Tips

- **Flavored Oil:** Nearly any type of quality oil, from olive to truffle to walnut oils, can be enhanced with a little help from some herbs and spices. This, in turn, enlivens the flavor of breads, salads or virtually whatever you are cooking that requires the use of oil.

- A 750-millimeter bottle with a cork (wine bottle) is a good way to store flavored oils. Allow oils to marinate over time to your desired taste, or serve them right away. (***Refrigerate all oil containing garlic** and use unbaked garlic oil within 1 week.)

- **Keep several cans of fruit in the refrigerator.** If you need to make a quick fruit salad, the fruit is already chilled.

- **When you run out of pickles** but still have juice left, slice a cucumber and pack it in the juice. Let it sit in the refrigerator at least 1 week before using.

- **Use kitchen shears to cut green onions or chives** for salads and to use in recipes. It is much safer and faster than using a knife.

- **To save time when preparing potato salad,** put the peeled cooked potatoes and peeled hard cooked eggs into a bowl and use a pastry blender to chop them.

To Make Sprouts

Place ¼ cup of mung beans in a quart jar and cover with tepid water. Cover with a cloth (such as a cheesecloth) and tie securely around the jar. Soak overnight. Drain off water. Set in a warm dark place.

Every day, rinse with tepid water and drain. Place in a warm dark place again. Repeat for four or five days until the sprouts are as big as you want.

Bean Salad

1   can whole corn
1   can green beans
1   can wax beans
1   cup green and red peppers, diced
½   cup celery, chopped
1   onion, chopped (or to taste)

Mix together and cover with dressing. Refrigerate at least 1 hour. This gets better the longer it sits. Serves 6.

Dressing

1   cup sugar
1   cup vinegar
½   cup vegetable oil
½   tsp. salt

Combine and shake well.

Carrot Salad

2   cups carrots, cooked but not mushy
1   cup chopped onion
½   cup chopped green peppers
1   stalk celery, chopped (optional)
1   cup sugar
½   cup oil
¼   cup vinegar
¼   tsp. Worcestershire sauce
½   tsp. mustard
1   cup tomato sauce

Mix all ingredients and refrigerate overnight before serving. Serves 4.

Cole Slaw

½   cup mayonnaise or dairy free salad dressing
¼   cup sugar
3   carrots, shredded
1   small head cabbage, shredded

Mix mayonnaise or salad dressing in a bowl with the sugar. Mix cabbage and carrots together. Add sauce to cabbage and carrots just before serving.

The dressing can be made in advance and stored in a separate container in the refrigerator. Serves 8.

Cucumber Salad

3   medium cucumbers, peeled and diced
½   medium onion, diced
1   Tbsp. white vinegar
⅓   cup sugar
¼   cup water

Mix all the ingredients in a bowl. Cover and refrigerate several hours or overnight. Serves 4.

Garden Salad

⅓   cup zucchini, sliced
⅓   cup fresh mushrooms, sliced
1   small tomato, sliced
⅓   cup green pepper, sliced
⅓   cup celery, sliced
⅓   cup green onions with tops, chopped
½   tsp. fresh basil, chopped

Combine all of the vegetables in a bowl. In a small bowl, whisk together the dressing ingredients. Pour over the salad and toss to coat. This recipe can be easily doubled or tripled. Serves 2-4.

Dressing

¼   cup olive or vegetable oil
2   Tbsp. red wine vinegar
¼   tsp. dried oregano
⅛   tsp. garlic powder
⅛   tsp. salt
⅛   tsp. pepper

Salad Topping

2   cups gluten free oats
½   cup dairy free butter, melted
⅓   cup dairy free Parmesan cheese, grated
1   tsp. oregano, dried
½   tsp. thyme, dried
¼   tsp. seasoned salt

Preheat oven to 350°. Mix all the ingredients in a bowl. Spread onto an ungreased 15x10x1 inch baking pan. Bake 15-18 minutes, until lightly browned. Cool. Store in an airtight container for up to 3 months. Makes 3 cups.

Garlic Salad

6-8 stalks celery
6-8 carrots
½   tsp. garlic powder
1½   tsp. garlic salt
1   pint Hellman's or Best Foods mayonnaise (no substitutes)

Place celery and carrots in a blender with a little water. Chop finely, drain and dry between two paper towels. Add garlic powder, garlic salt and mayonnaise. Mix well and chill overnight. Serves 6-8.

Macaroni Salad

6   cups gluten free macaroni, cooked
1   dill pickle, chopped (optional)
½   cup mayonnaise
2   hard boiled eggs, chopped (optional)
½   onion, finely chopped or 1 tsp. onion powder
2   stalks celery, diced
2   carrots, diced
1   tsp. garlic powder
     salt (to taste)
½   lb. chicken, turkey, or ham (optional)

Mix all the ingredients together and chill before serving. Simple but delicious. Serves 6-8.

Broccoli Salad

4   cups broccoli, cut into pieces
4   cups cauliflower, cut into pieces
2   cups celery, sliced
½   cup green olives, sliced
1   avocado, cut into small cubes
¼-½ cup sunflower seeds
      Italian dressing

Put everything into a bowl and sprinkle with Italian dressing, to taste.
You can have everything cut and ready the day before, except the
avocado and the dressing, and then add these items just before
serving.

Potato Salad

¼   cup mayonnaise
1   tsp. garlic powder (or more to taste)
1   tsp. onion powder or ½ onion, finely chopped (more to taste)
1   dill pickle, diced into small pieces
3   eggs, hard boiled and chopped
6   potatoes, peeled, cubed into small pieces and boiled
2   carrots, peeled and chopped
2   slices bacon, fried and crumbled or 1 Tbsp. bacon
        grease (optional)
      salt (to taste)

Mix the mayonnaise, garlic powder, onion powder and pickle in a large
bowl. Add eggs and warm potatoes, carrots and bacon, if desired, and
mix well. Add salt, to taste. Mix well. Chill 1-2 hours before serving.

If the potato salad seems dry, add a couple of tablespoons of milk.
Serves 10.

- **When making potato salad, add the dressing to warm
potatoes for the best taste. Warm potatoes will absorb the
flavor from the dressing while cool ones will not.**

Croutons

1½ tsp. garlic, minced
¼   tsp. salt and pepper (to taste)
¼   cup olive oil or vegetable oil
3   cups gluten free bread cubes*
2   tsp. dairy free Parmesan cheese (optional)
½   tsp. onion powder (or less to taste)
½   tsp. Italian seasoning (optional)

Preheat oven to 350°. In a small bowl, mix garlic, salt and pepper and olive oil.

Put bread cubes into a separate bowl and sprinkle with Parmesan cheese, onion powder and Italian seasoning, if desired. Pour the oil mixture over the bread cubes and toss.

Spread out on a baking sheet. Bake, turning once, until golden brown, about 15-20 minutes.

Store in an airtight container. These taste best if they are allowed to sit for one day before using. Makes 3 cups.

*Any thick pieces of leftover bread will work.

Deviled Eggs

6   hard boiled eggs
⅛   tsp. salt
¼   tsp. prepared mustard
⅓   cup mayonnaise
1   tsp. vinegar (optional)
    paprika
    parsley, chopped

Shell hard boiled eggs and cut in half. Remove the yolks and mash. Add salt, mustard, mayonnaise and vinegar (if using) and mix until smooth. Heap yolk mixture into whites and sprinkle with paprika or chopped parsley. Serves 6.

Garlic Deviled Eggs

Add 1 clove garlic, pressed, to egg yolk mixture in preceding recipe.

• **To stuff deviled eggs, put the filling in a resealable plastic bag. Cut off a small corner of the bag and squeeze the filling into the egg halves.**

Chile Garlic Oil

6   dried chilies of your choice
4   cloves garlic
4   cups 10% olive oil and 90% vegetable oil, or 100% olive oil

Preheat oven to 350°. Split chilies lengthwise.

Peel the garlic and slice into halves. Pour 2 tablespoons oil into a pie tin. Add the garlic and chilies and roast in an oven for 20 minutes, turning the chilies and garlic every 5 minutes.

Remove pie tin from the oven and allow to cool. Place the chilies, garlic and oil into a bottle. Then add remaining oil. Cork. Makes 4 cups.

*Refrigerate all oil containing garlic and use within 1 month.
Baking kills the spores that cause botulism.

> Sometimes an unanswered
> prayer is a blessing.

Italian Vinaigrette

½   cup red wine vinegar
1   cup olive oil or vegetable oil, or a combination
2   Tbsp. onion, finely chopped, or ¼ tsp. onion powder
2   large cloves garlic, crushed
¾   tsp. salt
¼   tsp. black pepper
1   Tbsp. parsley, minced
1   tsp. dry mustard
½   tsp. dried basil or oregano
1   tsp. sugar

Combine ingredients in a large jar with a tight lid. Shake well.
Makes 1½ cups.

For **Creamy Italian Dressing**, beat ½ cup mayonnaise into Italian
Vinaigrette.

For **Low-Calorie Vinaigrette**, substitute apple juice for the oil and
reduce vinegar to ⅓ cup.

Zesty Vinaigrette

¾   cup vegetable oil
¼   cup white wine vinegar
1   tsp. salt
1   tsp. dry mustard
½   tsp sugar
½   tsp garlic powder
3-4 drops Tabasco sauce

In a jar with a tight fitting lid, combine the ingredients and shake well.

Lemon Garlic Dressing

½   cup olive oil or vegetable oil
¼   cup lemon juice
½   tsp. salt
⅛   tsp. pepper
2   cloves garlic, split

Combine all ingredients in a jar with a tight lid and shake. Let stand at room temperature for 1 hour. Remove garlic before serving. Makes ¾ cup.

Lemon Pepper Dressing

1   cup plain or nonfat dairy free yogurt (soy)
1   Tbsp. parsley, chopped or 1½ tsp. dried parsley
1   Tbsp. lemon juice
¼   tsp. pepper
1   clove garlic, crushed or ¼ tsp. garlic powder

For herbed dressing, add:

1   tsp. fresh herbs or ¼ tsp. dried herbs (dill, oregano, basil, rosemary or tarragon)

Mix all ingredients and stir well. Refrigerate before serving. For a low fat dressing, use low fat yogurt. Makes 1 cup.

Old Fashioned Salad Dressing

2   cups sugar
2   Tbsp. cornstarch
1   tsp. salt
½   tsp. ground mustard
3   eggs, slightly beaten
1   cup vinegar
1   cup water
     mayonnaise

In a saucepan, combine sugar, cornstarch, salt and mustard. Stir in eggs. Gradually stir in vinegar and water until smooth. Bring to a boil over medium heat, stirring constantly. Cook and stir for 2 minutes. Cover and refrigerate.

Just before serving, combine the desired amount of dressing base with an equal amount of mayonnaise. Refrigerate leftovers. Tastes great on potato salad, coleslaw or salad greens. Makes 4 cups.

If you answer the phone with
"Hello you are on the air,"
most telemarketers will hang up.

Poppyseed Dressing

¾   cup sugar
1   tsp. dry mustard
1½   tsp. onion salt
⅓   cup vinegar
1   cup vegetable oil
1   Tbsp. poppy seeds

Mix sugar, mustard and onion salt. Add vinegar and mix well. Add oil slowly, beating with a mixer or blender constantly until thick. Add poppy seeds and beat until well blended.

Great on fruit salad. Makes 1½ cups.

Ranch Dressing

1   cup mayonnaise (low fat may be used)
1   cup dairy free milk (rice or soy)
1   Tbsp. onion flakes
½   tsp. oregano
¼   tsp. onion powder or 1 Tbsp. fresh onions, minced
1   tsp. dried parsley
¼   tsp. garlic powder or ½ to 1 clove garlic, finely minced
¼   tsp. paprika
⅛   tsp. cayenne pepper
¼   tsp. salt
¼   tsp. black pepper

Combine ingredients in a container with a lid and refrigerate before serving. Makes 2 cups.

For Ranch Dip, use dairy free sour cream.

Sweet Tomato French Dressing

(Tastes like Catalina Dressing)

⅔   cup ketchup
½   cup sugar (or to taste)
⅔   cup vegetable oil
½   cup lemon juice or vinegar
    salt (to taste)
1-2 cloves garlic, pressed
½   tsp. onion powder

Combine all ingredients in a jar with tight lid and shake. Refrigerate. Makes 2 cups.

Thousand Island Dressing

¾   cup mayonnaise
1   Tbsp. sweet pickle relish or sweet pickle, minced
2   Tbsp. chili sauce or ketchup
2   Tbsp. green bell peppers, minced
1   Tbsp. fresh or 1½ tsp. dried parsley
½   tsp. onion powder or 2 Tbsp. onion, minced
½   tsp. granulated sugar
¼   tsp. Worcestershire sauce
1   Tbsp. lemon juice
1   hard boiled egg, chopped

Combine all the ingredients in a bowl except the egg. Mix well. Stir in the egg. Refrigerate. Makes 1⅓ cups.

Dilled Onions

½ cup sugar
2 tsp. salt
¾ tsp. dill seeds
½ cup white vinegar
¼ cup water
6 white onions, sliced

In a saucepan, heat all the ingredients except the onions. Bring to a rolling boil. Add onions and let stand until cool. Store in covered jars in the refrigerator. Makes 2 cups.

Dilled Veggies

6-8 carrots, cut into sticks
cauliflower
bell peppers
leftover brine from dill pickles

Simmer carrots in salted water until not quite tender. Drain. Pour leftover pickle brine over the carrots and heat just until boiling. Cool and put into a jar.

Store in the refrigerator up to several weeks. You may use also cauliflower and peppers in place of or with carrots.

- **Store toothpicks in an empty spice bottle with a shaker top and screw-on lid. It's easy to remove the lid and gently shake out a toothpick through the holes when you need one.**

Garlic Pickles

4	(1 pint) jars
8	heads of dill
4	cloves garlic
8	Tbsp. pickling spices
1	hot pepper, cut into 4-5 pieces
12	cucumbers, sliced (4-5 inches long)
1	cup water
4	cups vinegar
½	cup salt, non-iodized

Place 2 heads of dill, 1 clove of garlic and 2 tablespoons of pickling spice into each jar. Add 1 piece of pepper to each jar. Pack sliced cucumbers into jars. Boil the last three ingredients and pour over the cucumbers.

Refrigerate several weeks before serving. Makes 4-5 pints.

Refrigerator Bread And Butter Pickles

4	cups sugar
4	cups vinegar
½	cup pickling salt
1⅓	tsp. turmeric
1⅓	tsp. celery seeds
1⅓	tsp. mustard
	cucumbers, sliced thin (as many as will fill your jar)
4	medium onions, sliced

Mix sugar, vinegar and spices in a bowl. Wash and sterilize 4 quart sized jars. Slice cucumbers to fill jars and add onions. Stir sugar mixture and pour over cucumbers and onions. Screw on lids and refrigerate 5 days before using. Makes 4 quarts.

Herb Dip

1   clove garlic
2   cups dairy free sour cream
¼   tsp. each dried basil, dill, marjoram, thyme and pepper
1   cup dairy free butter
1   tsp. dried oregano

Crush garlic and blend all ingredients together. You can store this in the refrigerator for up to a week. Makes 2 cups.

Vegetable Dip

1   cup mayonnaise
1   tsp. horseradish
1   tsp. dry mustard
1   tsp. curry powder
      dash of lemon juice
2   Tbsp. dairy free sour cream

Mix well and chill before serving. Serve with raw vegetables. Makes 1 cup.

Yogurt Dip

1   cup vanilla dairy free yogurt
2   Tbsp. brown sugar
1   (8 oz.) can crushed pineapple, drained
¼   cup coconut

Mix and refrigerate 1 hour or overnight. Great with fruit or dairy free cheese cubes. Makes 2 cups.

Meats And
Main Dishes

Meats And Main Dishes Tips

- **Cut the amount of meat in recipes by a half**, a quarter or a third. If a recipe calls for a pound of ground beef, use only half a pound.

- **Add 5 or 6 drops of lemon juice when boiling tough meat.** The juice will make the meat tender.

- **To make 3 meals out of 1 chicken:** Use the breast, thighs and drumsticks for fried chicken. Then boil the wings and the neck and make a broth. Remove the wings and the neck. Cool. Pick off any meat and return to the broth. Divide the broth in half and make Chicken and Dumplings (p.192) and Chicken Soup (p.103).

- **Leftover pineapple juice?** Add some oil, gluten free soy sauce and garlic. Mix well. Marinate chicken for several hours. Bake chicken in marinade until juices run clear.

- **Buy several hams at Easter** when they are on sale. Freeze and use all year.

- **Cook chicken breasts** with skin and remove skin just before eating. This helps the chicken stay juicy.

- **Finely chop any leftover meat** and use in spaghetti or pizza sauce.

- **Ask the butcher to cut your round steak** for you when it's on sale. Use for stews, fajitas, etc.

- **Cut your meat into smaller pieces.** It will go much further in stews and other recipes.

- **Save livers and gizzards** in a bag in the freezer. Add to them each time you cook a chicken or turkey. Then when you have enough, fry them. You can also use livers and gizzards for giblet gravy.

- **When using canned corned beef,** place the can in a saucepan with hot water for about 30 seconds. Then, when you open it, the corned beef will slip right out.

Beef Marinade

3   Tbsp. olive oil or salad oil
¼   cup gluten free soy sauce
¼   cup red wine vinegar
1   Tbsp. crushed rosemary
4   cloves garlic, minced (more or less to your taste)
    salt and pepper

Combine ingredients in a bowl. Place beef in a shallow pan. Pour marinade over beef. Marinate beef for 1 hour or overnight for best flavor.

When cooking the meat (whatever method you choose), put the excess marinade in a pan and simmer. If you want a thicker sauce, dissolve 1 tablespoon cornstarch in 1½ tablespoons water and add to simmering marinade. Use this as a sauce on the side.

Variations

- Substitute balsamic vinegar for soy sauce and red wine vinegar.

- Substitute ginger for the rosemary for a teriyaki flavor.

- Substitute rice wine vinegar or lemon juice for red wine vinegar.

- Add some sugar or honey for sweetness.

- Add Worcestershire sauce or chili powder for a different flavor.

Barbecued Meatballs

3   lbs. ground beef
2   cups gluten free oatmeal
2   eggs
1   tsp. onion powder or 1 Tbsp. onion, finely chopped
1   cup dairy free milk (rice or soy)
2   tsp. salt
2   tsp. chili powder
½   tsp. pepper

Preheat oven to 350°. Mix all the ingredients in a bowl and blend well. Form hamburger mixture into balls. Put into a 9x13 inch pan and an 8x8 inch pan and pour barbecue sauce over them. Bake 1 hour. Makes 30 medium meatballs.

Barbecue Sauce

1½ cups brown sugar
2   cups ketchup
½   tsp. garlic powder
2   Tbsp. liquid smoke

Combine all the ingredients in a bowl. Mix well. Sauce may be refrigerated several weeks.

Beef Jerky

1   lb. flank or round steak
1   tsp. seasoned salt
½   tsp. garlic powder
½   tsp. onion powder
¼   tsp. pepper
⅓   cup gluten free soy sauce
⅓   cup Worcestershire sauce
2   Tbsp. liquid smoke

Pat the steak dry with a paper towel. Slice thinly across the grain. In a bowl, combine the rest of the ingredients.

Place the meat in the bowl, making sure each slice is coated with marinade. Place in the refrigerator overnight. Drain meat on paper towels, blotting well.

Place meat on oven rack and cook at 140° for 3 hours, or in a food dehydrator for 8 hours. Store in a jar in the refrigerator.

Beef And Noodles

1   cup water
¼   cup cornstarch
1   lb. leftover roast
1   tsp. garlic powder
     salt and pepper (to taste)
1   lb. gluten free noodles, cooked

Mix water and cornstarch in a bowl and mix well. Pour into a saucepan and boil until it starts to thicken. Add roast. Cook until roast is heated through. Add garlic powder, salt and pepper. Serve over cooked noodles or on toast. Serves 6.

Barbecued Beef

leftover roast beef
3   Tbsp. water
barbecue sauce

Put leftover beef in a saucepan and add water. Cook over medium heat until warmed through. Add enough barbecue sauce to coat beef and simmer for 3 minutes. Serve on buns, bread or toast.

Barbecued Ribs

Place as many ribs as will fit into your crockpot and cover with barbecue sauce. Let simmer all day on low, basting every few hours. These will be the best ribs you have ever eaten. Serve with cornbread and cole slaw.

It must have taken a lot of courage
to discover that frog legs are edible.

Chicken Fried Steak

1   cup gluten free all purpose flour
     salt and pepper (to taste)
1   tsp. onion powder
     gluten free cracker crumbs
2   cloves garlic, crushed and chopped
1   lb. ground beef
½   cup dairy free milk (rice or soy)
1   egg, lightly beaten
     vegetable oil, for frying

Put some gluten free flour in a bowl with salt, pepper and onion powder. Put cracker crumbs in another bowl. Stir garlic into ground beef. Form into patties and smash flat. Combine milk and egg in a bowl. Dip each patty into flour, then into the egg/milk mixture and then into the cracker crumbs.

Fry in hot oil until golden brown on each side. Serve with white gravy. Serves 4.

White Gravy

2-4 Tbsp. drippings from chicken fried steak
4   Tbsp. cornstarch
2   cups dairy free milk (rice or soy)
     salt and pepper (to taste)

After frying the chicken fried steak, leave 2-4 tablespoons of drippings and crumbs in the pan. Add the cornstarch to 4 tablespoons water. Add to drippings quickly, stirring constantly until all the crumbs are loosened and mixture is thick.

Then add milk and boil until thickened. Add more or less milk, depending on the consistency you like. Salt and pepper to taste. Pour over chicken fried steak.

Fajitas

1½ lbs. round steak, beef chuck or chicken
½   cup lime juice
2   jalapeno peppers, seeded and finely chopped
1   clove garlic, minced
1   tsp. vegetable oil
6   corn tortillas, warmed

Salsa

1   large tomato, chopped
1   small onion, chopped
1   Tbsp. fresh cilantro

Cut meat crosswise into ½ inch thick strips. Pound each piece to ¼ inch thickness. Combine lime juice, jalapenos and garlic.

Place meat in a plastic bag. Add lime juice mixture, turning to coat the meat. Close bag securely. Marinate in the refrigerator 4-6 hours, turning occasionally.

Combine tomato, onion and cilantro for salsa. Cover tightly. Refrigerate.

Remove meat from marinade and discard marinade.

Heat oil in a large skillet on high. Cook meat pieces, 2 at a time, in hot oil for 2-3 minutes, turning once. Season with salt and pepper.

Serve meat slices in warm tortillas with salsa. Top with dairy free Cheddar cheese, if desired. Serves 6.

- **Eat by candlelight with tablecloths and place mats. It makes even plain meals look special.**

Tacos

½   lb. ground beef
     salt and pepper (to taste)
1-3 Tbsp. taco seasoning (p.320)
8   corn tortillas
     hot oil
     lettuce, chopped
     tomatoes, chopped
     dairy free cheese, grated
     onion, chopped

Brown ground beef with salt, pepper and taco seasoning. Drain well. Fry tortillas in hot oil. Drain on paper towels, either flat or folded. Fill with meat mixture. Add lettuce and tomatoes. Top with grated cheese and onions. Serve immediately. Serves 4.

Burritos

Refried beans (p.139)
gluten free or corn tortillas, warmed
dairy free sour cream (optional)
ground beef, browned
taco seasoning (p.320, optional)
olives (optional)
salsa (optional)
dairy free cheese, grated

Spoon beans onto tortillas. Add your choice of other ingredients, if desired. Top with grated cheese. Roll and tuck ends. Serve warm.

Bean Goulash

½   lb. ground beef
½   lb. bacon, chopped
1   stalk celery
1   small onion
1   (15 oz.) can kidney beans or 2 cups cooked beans
1   (15 oz.) can butter beans
1   (15 oz.) can pork and beans
1   Tbsp. vinegar
½   tsp. dry mustard
½   cup barbecue sauce or ketchup
½   cup sugar
½   cup brown sugar

Preheat oven to 350°. Brown ground beef, bacon, celery and onion. If using canned beans, drain them. Mix the rest of the ingredients together with ground beef mixture. Bake 30 minutes or put in the crockpot on low for 1-2 hours. Serves 8-10.

Hash

½   lb. ground beef
1   large onion, chopped
1   large green pepper, chopped
1   (16 oz.) can tomatoes, chopped
½   cup white rice, uncooked
2   tsp. chili powder
2   tsp. salt
⅛   tsp. pepper

Preheat oven to 350°. In a large skillet, brown beef, onion, and green pepper. Drain fat. Add tomatoes, rice, chili powder, salt and pepper. Heat through. Pour into a 2 quart casserole. Cover and bake 1 hour. Serves 4.

Slow Cooked Roast

1   beef roast, 3-5 lbs.
    seasoned salt
1   onion, sliced
1   cup water

Preheat oven to 250°. Place the roast in a pan. Sprinkle seasoned salt and onion on top. Add water to pan. Cover tightly. Bake 1 hour. Then turn down to 225° and cook for 15 or more hours or 10 hours for roasts smaller than 3 pounds. If you can shred it with a fork, it's done.

- **This recipe is excellent for inexpensive roasts.** It makes them so tender they fall off the bone and are almost impossible to lift out of the pan. It is excellent for Sunday after church or for guests, because it can cook for 2 or 3 hours longer without overcooking. Serves 4.

- **Use a meat thermometer** to make sure internal temperature reaches 145°.

Brown Gravy

    meat broth
1   Tbsp. cornstarch
1   cup cold water
    salt and pepper

Add at least one or two cups of water to the roasting pan of your roast, pork or chicken while the meat is cooking. Remove the meat when done and skim off the fat.

Put the roasting pan on a stovetop burner over medium heat.

Put cornstarch in a bowl. Add cold water. Stir until all the lumps are gone. Pour the mixture slowly into the simmering broth and stir constantly until thickened. If there is a lot of liquid you may need to use more cornstarch. Salt and pepper to taste. Serves 4.

Spanish Pot Roast

3-4 lb. pot roast
1   cup Catalina dressing (p.167)
¾   cup water
8   small onions
8   small potatoes
2   Tbsp. cornstarch

Cook the meat in a Dutch oven on medium-high heat in dressing and ½ cup water. Cover and simmer 3 hours on medium-low heat.

Add onions and potatoes. Continue simmering 45 minutes or until vegetables and meat are tender.

Remove meat and vegetables. Gradually add remaining water and cornstarch to a bowl. Stir until blended. Add cornstarch mixture to hot liquid in pan. Cook until mixture boils and thickens, stirring constantly. Simmer 3 minutes. Serve gravy over hot meat and vegetables. Serves 4.

Meatloaf

1½ lbs. ground beef
1   cup dairy free milk (rice or soy)
½   tsp. salt
½   tsp. dry mustard
¼   tsp. pepper
¾   cup gluten free oatmeal or
        ½ cup dry gluten free bread crumbs
1   egg
¼   tsp. garlic powder
1   tsp. onion powder
1   Tbsp. Worcestershire sauce
½   cup ketchup or barbecue sauce

Preheat oven to 350°. Mix everything together except ketchup. Put into a loaf pan. Spread ketchup over the top. Bake 1 hour or until done. Serves 6.

Shepherd's Pie

½   lb. ground beef
1   onion, chopped
2   carrots, diced
1   can peas, drained or
          1 can mixed vegetables for carrots and peas
1   (15 oz.) can tomato sauce
      salt and pepper (to taste)
1   tsp. sugar
2   tsp. onion powder
1   tsp. garlic powder
1   tsp. chili powder
4   cups mashed potatoes (p.128)
¾   cup grated dairy free Cheddar cheese

Brown ground beef and onion. Add carrots and cook until tender. Drain grease and add peas.

Preheat oven to 350°. In a casserole dish, combine tomato sauce, salt, pepper, sugar, onion powder, garlic powder and chili powder. Mix well and add the beef mixture. Mix again thoroughly. Top with mashed potatoes and then grated cheese.

Bake, uncovered, for 15 minutes or until the cheese melts. Serves 4.

- **To freeze 1 lb. portions of browned ground beef** or one or two chicken parts, place in a bread bag. Above each section, tie with a twist tie or make a knot, dividing into ½ lb. or 1 lb. portions. Freeze. Then, as needed, cut off each section above the knot.

- **When shaping hamburger patties,** poke a hole through the center of each one with your index finger. The burgers cook faster this way, and the outside doesn't get overcooked before the center is done. The holes disappear as the burgers cook.

Steak And Mushroom Gravy

1   Tbsp. dairy free butter
½   onion, chopped
5   Tbsp. cornstarch
    salt and pepper (to taste)
2   cups water
1-2 cups leftover beef
1   tsp. beef bouillon powder
1   small can mushroom pieces, drained

Melt butter in a large skillet and sauté onion. Mix cornstarch, salt and pepper in a bowl. Add water and stir until smooth. Stir into onions until simmering and thickened. Add beef, bouillon powder and drained mushrooms. Reduce the heat. Simmer, stirring constantly, until heated through. Serve over gluten free noodles, rice, mashed potatoes or gluten free toast. Serves 4.

Liver And Onions

2-4 slices bacon
1   lb. liver
1   onion, sliced
1   tsp. salt
    dash of pepper

Fry bacon in a large skillet. When crisp, remove and set aside, leaving grease in skillet.

Place liver in a skillet and fry in hot bacon grease over medium heat. Turn when browned. Fry 5-8 minutes until crisp and golden. Remove to platter. Add a small amount of oil to the skillet if necessary.

Add onion and fry briefly, just until lightly browned. Sprinkle with salt and pepper. When onion rings begin to wilt, remove and spread over liver. Arrange crisp bacon on top and serve with ketchup. Serves 4-6.

Swiss Steak

2	Tbsp. gluten free all purpose flour
½	tsp. salt
	dash of pepper
2	lbs. round steak
1	Tbsp. oil
1	medium onion, chopped
2-3	stalks celery, chopped
¼	cup green pepper, chopped
1	cup tomatoes, peeled
2	carrots, sliced (optional)
2	cups water
8	potatoes, boiled or mashed (optional)

Mix flour, salt and pepper in small bowl. Rub into round steak. Cut into serving sized pieces. Brown meat in oil in a skillet over medium heat.

Pour all vegetables except potatoes over steak and add water. Cover and reduce heat to low. Simmer 1 to 1½ hours or all day on low in the crockpot. Serve over potatoes, if desired. Serves 4.

- **Don't serve the entire roast. Save some for barbecue beef, beef and noodles, etc. Use only a small amount of meat on buns for barbecue beef.**

- **A Dutch oven is the same as a 6 or 8 quart saucepan in recipes.**

- **To add garlic to meat: Slice garlic clove thin. Make some slits in the top of the meat and place garlic slivers in the slits. Roast, broil or bake as usual.**

Roast Turkey

1   turkey, 20-22 lbs.
½   cup dairy free butter

Defrost frozen turkey for several days in the refrigerator, according to the directions on the package. Line a roasting pan with aluminum foil. Remove the insides of the turkey and save for giblet gravy or for fried livers and gizzards.

Preheat oven to 250°. Lay turkey, breast side down, in the pan and place the butter on the inside. Cover tightly with aluminum foil. Bake 1 hour. Reduce heat to 200° and roast for 10-14 hours or more.

The cooking time can be longer to fit your schedule. Test with a meat thermometer to make sure the temperature in the thigh is 180°.

This is the best turkey you will ever eat. The meat will just fall off the bones, so you will have to serve it already carved. It will be very juicy and moist.

- **Have the butcher cut your turkey in half for you when it's on sale. Then you don't have to cook the whole thing at once and waste it. Most butchers will do it for free.**

- **Save the bones from a turkey or chicken for soup.**

- **Don't buy a turkey with added ingredients, such as butter. Simply add your own.**

Turkey Gravy

3-4 cups turkey juices/drippings
2-4 Tbsp. cornstarch
½   cup water
     salt and pepper (to taste)

Pour turkey juices/drippings into a saucepan. Whisk cornstarch into ½ cup water. Add to drippings. Add salt and pepper. Simmer for about 15 minutes, stirring once in a while until it is the right consistency.

If the gravy is too strong or if you need to stretch it just a little, you can add a small amount of water.

Giblet Gravy

      livers and gizzards from turkey, chopped
      turkey drippings or broth
1   Tbsp. cornstarch
1   cup cold water
1   hard boiled egg, chopped
      salt and pepper

Boil livers and gizzards until cooked through. Pour 2-3 cups turkey broth into a saucepan. Add 1 cup additional water if more gravy is needed. Skim off the fat. Put the pan on a stovetop burner on medium heat. Simmer.

Put cornstarch in a bowl with cold water. Mix until lumps are gone. Pour slowly into the simmering broth and stir constantly, until thickened. If there is a lot of liquid, you may need to use more cornstarch.

Stir in egg, livers and gizzards. Salt and pepper to taste.

Chicken And Dumplings

4   cups chicken broth
½-1½ cups chicken or turkey, cooked
½   cup celery, sliced
½   cup carrots, sliced
1   bay leaf
1   tsp. parsley flakes

Dumplings

¾   cup gluten free all purpose **baking mix***
½   tsp. baking powder
¼   tsp. dried thyme, optional
1   tsp. dried parsley, optional
⅓   cup dairy free milk (rice or soy)
2   Tbsp. dairy free butter, melted
1   egg

In a Dutch oven, combine broth, chicken, celery, carrots, bay leaf and parsley. Bring to a boil.

In a bowl, combine baking mix, baking powder, thyme and parsley. Stir in milk, butter and egg, just until moistened. Drop by tablespoonfuls into the boiling broth.

Cover and cook 15 minutes.

DO NOT PEEK or your dumplings will be soggy. Remove dumplings with a slotted spoon and serve in bowls. Remove bay leaf and spoon broth over the top of the dumplings. Serves 4.

*Make **SURE** it's **baking mix** and **NOT** gluten free all purpose flour.

Chicken And Pasta

1	lb. fresh spinach, rinsed well
1	cup chicken broth
1	(16 oz.) pkg. gluten free pasta shells
1	tsp. olive oil or vegetable spray
4	cloves garlic, minced
½	tsp. nutmeg or mace
	salt and pepper
½	lb. chicken breast, boned, skinned, grilled and cut into 1 inch pieces
½	cup dairy free Parmesan cheese, grated

Cook the spinach in the broth until tender. Drain and reserve broth. Remove excess liquid by mashing. Cook pasta.

In a heavy skillet over medium heat, add the oil or vegetable spray and sauté the garlic, stirring constantly, until it is white (about 1 minute). Don't allow it to brown.

Add the spinach, nutmeg or mace and salt and pepper. Add the chicken pieces to the spinach. Stir and add a small amount of the reserved cooking broth. Stir the spinach until it is hot. If the spinach starts to get dry, add broth as necessary.

Add the cooked pasta to the spinach mixture and blend well. Serve immediately with Parmesan cheese sprinkled on top. Serves 4.

If you would like your house to be clean,

invite someone over to dinner.

Chicken Wings And Easy Barbecue Sauce

¼ cup grape or other jelly
¼ cup ketchup
    garlic, to taste
1   lb. chicken wings

Preheat oven to 350°. Mix jelly, ketchup and garlic to make barbecue sauce. Spread chicken wings on a cookie sheet and spoon half or a little more of the barbecue sauce over the chicken wings.

Bake 20 minutes. Turn and baste with the remaining sauce. Bake for another 20 minutes.

Save the wings from your fryer packs until you have a good amount, then make this recipe. Serves 4.

Hot Wings

12 chicken wings
½   cup dairy free butter, melted
1   cup hot sauce
    oil for frying
    dairy free ranch dressing (p.166)

Cut the tips off the chicken wings. In a large saucepan, heat the oil to 350°. Place the wings in the pot. Do not crowd. Fry until golden and crispy, about 10 minutes.

Combine butter and hot sauce. Toss wings in half of the butter sauce. Serve with dressing and the extra butter sauce for dipping.

Makes 12 wings. This recipe may be doubled or tripled.

Italian Chicken

4-8 pieces chicken
     lemon pepper
1   onion, sliced
2   cups Italian dressing

Preheat oven to 350°. Place the chicken in a greased baking dish. Sprinkle with lemon pepper. Add onion and cover with Italian salad dressing. Bake about 1 hour or until the chicken is done. Serves 4-6.

Grilled Italian Chicken

Marinate the chicken in Italian dressing for several hours. Then place on a hot grill. Cook until the juices run clear.

Honey Baked Chicken

This has been our #1 readers' favorite recipe
on our website for 20 years!

6   chicken fryer pieces
⅓   cup dairy free butter, melted
⅓   cup honey
2   Tbsp. prepared mustard
1   tsp. salt

Preheat oven to 350°. Arrange chicken in a baking dish with the skin side up. Combine the rest of the ingredients and pour over chicken. Bake 1 hour and 15 minutes, basting every 15 minutes (until chicken is tender and brown). Serve with rice. Serves 4-6.

Lemony Chicken Breast

2   bell peppers, chopped
1   whole chicken breast, boneless and skinless
1   Tbsp. cornstarch
½   tsp. salt
½   tsp. pepper
2   tsp. olive oil
2   cups gluten free pasta, cooked
⅓   cup chicken broth
2   Tbsp. lemon juice
1   Tbsp. parsley, chopped

In a skillet, sauté bell peppers over medium heat in a small amount of oil. Cut chicken into strips.

Mix cornstarch, salt and pepper in a bowl. Coat chicken with cornstarch mixture. Remove peppers.

Heat oil in the skillet, still on medium heat. Add chicken and cook 6-8 minutes, until brown. Add peppers and warm. Put pasta on a serving dish. Place chicken and peppers on pasta.

Add chicken broth and lemon juice to skillet. Stir over medium heat 2-3 minutes. Scrape brown bits on the bottom of the pan and cook until reduced. Stir in parsley. Pour over chicken. Serves 2.

Maple Glazed Chicken

¼   cup maple syrup
4   tsp. lemon juice
1   Tbsp. dairy free butter
4   pieces chicken
     salt and pepper (to taste)

Preheat oven to 450°. Mix maple syrup, lemon juice and butter together in a small saucepan. Simmer for 5 minutes.

Spray a baking dish and place chicken in it. Salt and pepper the chicken. Bake 10 minutes.

Remove from oven and pour on glaze. Bake for 15 minutes more or until juices run clear. Serves 4.

Mexican Chicken

4-6 pieces chicken (remove skin)
1   cup salsa
      grated dairy free Cheddar cheese (to taste)

Preheat oven to 350°. Place chicken in a baking dish and top with salsa. Cover. Bake about 45 minutes or until done. Sprinkle grated dairy free Cheddar cheese on top and serve. Great over rice. Serves 4-6.

Oven Fried Chicken

¼   cup dairy free butter
6   pieces chicken
1-1½ cups gluten free baking mix
        salt and pepper (to taste)

Preheat oven to 375°. Melt dairy free butter in a 9x13 inch pan. Dip chicken pieces in melted butter. Then roll or shake in baking mix, until coated. Return to the 9x13 inch pan.

Bake uncovered, skin side down, for 50 minutes. Turn the chicken and bake 15 more minutes or until the chicken is done. Serves 4-6.

Mushroom Chicken

1   chicken, cut into pieces
        gluten free all purpose flour
2   cups water
1   tsp. chicken bouillon
        bay leaf
1   tsp. onion salt
½-¾ cup mushrooms
¼   tsp. thyme
¾   cup dairy free sour cream

Preheat oven to 350°. Place chicken in a plastic bag with some gluten free flour and shake to coat the chicken in flour. Place in a greased 9x13 inch pan.

Mix the water, bouillon, bay leaf, onion salt and mushrooms. Pour over the chicken. Cover and bake 2 hours.

In the last 15 minutes of baking, add the thyme and sour cream and continue baking. Leave the foil off for that last 15 minutes.

Roast Chicken

1   chicken
1-2 cloves garlic
1   tsp. thyme (to taste)
1   tsp. rosemary (to taste)
1   tsp. oregano (to taste)
     olive oil
     salt and pepper

Preheat oven to 450°. Rub the inside of the chicken with garlic cloves. Put thyme, rosemary and oregano, to taste, inside the bird. Rub the outside of the bird with olive oil, salt and pepper.

Bake 15 minutes. Then turn the oven down to 400° and roast for 35-45 minutes (for a 2½ pound bird) or 1 hour (for a 3-5 pound bird) or until the temperature of the thigh reaches 180°. Allow to rest 10 minutes before serving. Serves 6-8.

Recipe for a Happy Marriage

1 cup consideration
2 cups flattery, carefully concealed
2 cups milk of human kindness
1 gallon faith in God and in each other
1 reasonable budget, mixed with a generous dash of cooperation
1 cup each confidence and encouragement
2 cups praise
1 small pinch in-laws
3 teaspoons pure extract of "I'm sorry"
1 cup contentment
1 large or 2 small hobbies
1 cup of blindness to the other's faults

For extra flavor, add recreation and a dash of happy memories. Stir well and remove any specks of jealousy, temper or criticism. If you like a sweeter product, add a generous portion of Love. Keep warm with a steady flame of devotion. Never serve with a cold shoulder or a hot tongue. Add to the recipe the presence and love of God and you will have quite a home.

Stir Fry

3 Tbsp. peanut butter
2 Tbsp. gluten free soy sauce
½ tsp. hot sauce
1 Tbsp. cornstarch
1 cup water
1 Tbsp. oil
3-4 slices ginger root, peeled and minced
2 cloves garlic, mashed, or 1 tsp. garlic powder
2 stalks celery, sliced
2 onions, sliced
2 green peppers, sliced
2 cups cabbage, shredded
½ cup leftover beef, turkey or chicken
2 Tbsp. water

In a bowl, mix peanut butter, soy sauce and hot sauce. Stir cornstarch into 1 cup of water. Add to bowl.

In a deep skillet, simmer ginger and garlic in oil over medium heat. Add vegetables, starting with the firmest, as you dice the others. Stir after each addition and sprinkle on water as needed. Make sure you do not overcook the vegetables. Add cooked meat last.

Push vegetables to the side and add sauce to the pot while stirring. Add additional water if needed. As the sauce clears, mix in the vegetables. Serve over rice. Serves 4.

• **Peel the whole fresh ginger root and freeze. Then grate as needed and return to the freezer. Stays fresh for several months this way.**

Slow Cooked Ham

1   ham

Preheat oven to 250°. Cover the bottom of a roasting pan with aluminum foil. Bake ham 1 hour. Reduce the heat to 200° and roast another 12-15 hours.

This recipe is great because you can put in the oven overnight and it will be ready the next day for the noon meal. The cooking time can go for longer, if needed, to fit your schedule, since it cooks at such a low temperature. Serves 4-6.

Spiced Honey Ham

½   cup mustard
½   cup brown sugar
¼   cup honey
¼   cup orange juice
1   tsp. cloves
1   Slow Cooked Ham

Mix first 5 ingredients. Score the top of the Slow Cooked Ham. Pour the mixture over the ham. Bake according to the slow cooked ham directions. Baste with ham juices every half hour. Serves 4-6.

Ham And Beans

2   cups dried lima beans or great northern beans, washed well
1   tsp. salt
⅛   tsp. pepper
2   cups ham, cubed in pieces

Soak beans overnight in 6 cups of water. Drain and put in pot with 6 cups fresh water. Season with salt and pepper. Add ham and simmer over low heat for 2-3 hours or until beans are tender. Serves 6-8. This recipe is great with cornbread.

Sweet Pork Chops

4   pork chops
     salt (to taste)
1   onion, sliced, or a sprinkle of onion powder
4   Tbsp. ketchup
½   cup sweet pickle juice

Preheat oven to 350°. Arrange pork chops in a baking pan. Sprinkle with salt and top each with 1 slice onion and 1 tablespoon ketchup. Pour the pickle juice around the pork chops. Cover and bake 1 hour. Serves 4.

Peachy Pork Chops

4   pork chops
½   cup peach jam
1   Tbsp. vinegar
1½ tsp. mustard
½   tsp. Worcestershire sauce
     dash Tabasco sauce

In a frying pan, brown meat and cook until done. Combine the rest of the ingredients. Heat in a saucepan and serve over meat. Serves 4.

- **To prevent salt and pepper shakers from leaking while you're filling them, place a piece of tape over the holes. Once they're filled, turn upright and remove the tape.**

Green Chile

½-1   lb. pork roast, pork chops or chicken,
        meat removed, cubed into small pieces
10½ oz. chicken broth
1   onion, finely chopped
¼-½ tsp. garlic powder
1   (7 oz.) can green chilies, diced
¼   jalapeno, finely chopped
1   Tbsp. dairy free butter
1   tsp. salt
1   Tbsp. cornstarch, dissolved in 2 Tbsp. water
      corn tortillas

Toppings

dairy free Cheddar cheese, grated
lettuce, shredded
tomato
dairy free sour cream

Simmer pork in broth on low for 10 minutes.

Add all other ingredients except cornstarch and tortillas and simmer 45 minutes. Thicken with cornstarch until it is like a thick soup.

Spoon about ¼ cup into the center of a corn tortilla. Roll up tortilla and top with more green chile. Sprinkle with cheese, lettuce and tomato. Top with sour cream if desired. This green chile freezes really well. Serves 4.

- **Ever cook a dish and found it too spicy for your taste? Add sugar, 1 tablespoon at a time, tasting after each addition. This helps cut the "fire" in spicy foods.**

Quesadillas

1   (7 oz.) can green chiles (optional)
     salsa (optional)
½-1 lb. dairy free cheese, shredded
12   corn tortillas
     dairy free butter

Place ½-1 teaspoon green chiles (to taste) or 1 tablespoon salsa on 1-2 tablespoons of cheese in the center of each tortilla. Fold tortilla over cheese and pin shut with a toothpick. Melt butter in a skillet and fry until crisp, turning occasionally. Drain on paper towels. Serves 6.

Stacked Enchiladas

½   lb. ground beef
1   onion, chopped, or 1 tsp. onion powder
2½   cups gluten free enchilada sauce (p.206)
8   corn tortillas
     vegetable oil, for frying
1   cup dairy free Cheddar cheese, grated
1   tomato, chopped
2   cups lettuce, chopped
     dairy free sour cream (optional)
     olives (optional)

In a skillet, brown ground beef and onion. Drain on paper towels. Add enchilada sauce and set aside.

Heat ½ inch oil in a small skillet. (Oil is hot when a tortilla sizzles when dropped in the skillet.) To soften tortillas, dip one tortilla in hot oil for 5 seconds, turn and then remove softened tortilla to a paper towel. Soften all tortillas, draining on paper towel before stacking.

Place one tortilla on a serving plate. Place ¼ cup of the beef mixture on top of tortilla. Add another tortilla and repeat stacking, ending with beef mixture on top.

Add shredded cheese, tomato, lettuce, sour cream and olives. Serve warm. Serves 4.

Beef Enchiladas

6-8 corn tortillas, warm
1   cup ground beef, cooked
½   cup dairy free cheese, shredded
½   onion, chopped
1   clove garlic, crushed
1   can of gluten free enchilada sauce or homemade (see below)

Preheat oven to 350°. Mix ground beef, cheese, onion and garlic. Place enchilada sauce in a bowl. Dip 1 tortilla into sauce. Place in a greased 9x9 inch pan. Spoon about ¼ cup cheese mixture down the center of each tortilla. Roll up and tuck in ends. Place into pan, seam sides down. Repeat with rest of tortillas.

Top with the remaining enchilada sauce and sprinkle cheese on top.

Bake, covered, until cheese is melted and bubbly (about 40 minutes). Serves 4.

Enchilada Sauce

1   (15 oz.) can tomato sauce
1   Tbsp. chili powder
5   Tbsp. green pepper, chopped (optional)
1   tsp. onion powder
½   tsp. dried oregano
½   tsp. salt (more to taste)
1   tsp. garlic powder
¼   tsp. cumin

Combine all ingredients in a saucepan, mixing well. Cook and stir over medium heat until thickened. Makes 2 cups.

Pizza

2 crust	1 crust	
1½	¾	cups warm water (110-115°)
2	1	Tbsp. sugar
4	3	tsp. yeast
4	2	cups gluten free all purpose flour
2	1	tsp. salt
2	1	eggs
2	1	Tbsp. oil
2	1	tsp. apple cider vinegar
1	½	tsp. garlic powder (optional)
1	½	tsp. Italian seasoning (optional)

Place baking sheet in oven and preheat to 450°.

Mix water, sugar and yeast in a medium mixing bowl and stir. Let stand 5 minutes until foaming.

Add flour, salt, egg, oil, vinegar and spices, if using. Mix with a mixer on low for 1 minute until well combined. Dough will be sticky.

Spray parchment paper with cooking oil. If making two crusts, prepare 2 pieces of parchment paper.

Spray fingers with cooking oil. If making two crusts, divide dough in half and place one half on each piece of parchment paper. Spread dough into a 10-12 inch round or rectangle and pat into shape using well oiled fingers.

Bake 8-10 minutes.

Add toppings and cheese and bake 8-10 more minutes.

• **Instead of a traditional tomato sauce, brush the crust with a mixture of olive oil and minced garlic. Then top as usual.**

Toppings

pizza sauce (p.210)
½ lb. DF mozzarella cheese, grated
pepperoni
onions
olives
green peppers
mushrooms
sausage
ground beef, browned

Garden Vegetable Pizza

Thinly sliced zucchini, diced tomato, mushrooms, onions and bell pepper

Greek Pizza

Black olives, artichoke hearts, red onion, and DF feta cheese

Hawaiian Pizza

Ham or Canadian bacon and pineapple

Meat Pizza

Sausage, salami, Italian sausage, Canadian bacon. Choose any or all meats you enjoy.

Barbecue Chicken Pizza

Spread with barbecue sauce. Top with barbecue chicken, DF mozzarella, red onion and cilantro.

Garden Pizza Or Spaghetti Sauce

6   onions, finely chopped
3   green peppers, finely chopped
¾   cup vegetable oil or olive oil
½   tsp. black pepper
18   tomatoes, skinned or stewed tomatoes, chopped
2   cloves garlic, minced
1½   Tbsp. salt
2   Tbsp. sugar
1   Tbsp. oregano
1   Tbsp.basil
1   Tbsp.thyme
6   bay leaves
3   (12 oz.) cans tomato paste
1   cup beef stock or bouillon (optional)

Sauté onions and green pepper in vegetable oil in a Dutch oven. Add black pepper. Add tomatoes, garlic, salt, sugar, and herbs to the pot. Bring to a boil. Add tomato paste, one can at a time, and beef stock, if using. Simmer on low for 1 hour to reduce. Freeze in 1 quart bags. Makes 4 quarts.

How To Cut Down On Meat

Have meat two nights per week
Eat soup and a sandwich once a week
Have a pasta or rice night twice a week
Have a "leftovers" day
Have a baked potato night

Polish Sausage

2	lbs. pork butt, coarsely ground
¾	lb. beef, finely ground
1½	tsp. coarse salt
1½	tsp. peppercorns, crushed
1½	tsp. marjoram
1	Tbsp. paprika
1	tsp. garlic powder
1½	tsp. sugar (optional)
½	tsp. ground nutmeg

Sprinkle the seasonings over the ground meat. Knead until thoroughly blended. Make into patties. Refrigerate in airtight containers for 2 to 3 days to allow flavors to blend. Fry until golden brown. Freeze any unused sausage. Serves 4-6.

Breakfast Sausage

1	lb. ground pork or beef
¼-1	tsp. sage (to taste)
¼–½	tsp. marjoram
¼–½	tsp. thyme (optional)
1	tsp. salt
⅛	tsp. pepper
1-3	Tbsp. water

Prepare using the instructions for Polish Sausage (above).

• **When you finish grinding meat, run a piece of bread through the meat grinder. This will make it easier to clean.**

Italian Sausage

1 lb. ground pork or ½ lb. ground pork and ½ lb. ground beef
1 onion, minced
1½ tsp. salt
1 clove garlic, minced
1 tsp. basil
½ tsp. pepper
½ tsp. dried oregano
¼ tsp. paprika
⅛ tsp. thyme
1 tsp. cayenne pepper
1 tsp. fennel seeds

Prepare using the instructions for Polish Sausage (p.211).

Salami

2-2½ lbs. ground beef
½ tsp. onion powder
½ tsp. garlic powder
2 Tbsp. curing salt
1 Tbsp. mustard seeds
1½ tsp. liquid smoke
¾ cup water
   pinch of crushed red pepper

Mix all the ingredients together. Shape into three rolls on foil and wrap securely. Refrigerate 24 hours.

Preheat oven to 300°. Open foil and bake 1 hour and 15 minutes. Makes 3 rolls.

Baked Fish And Vegetables

4   fish fillets
4   medium potatoes, cut into 1 inch cubes
4   medium carrots, cut into 1 inch pieces
4   small onions, quartered
4   Tbsp. dairy free butter
     salt, pepper, garlic powder, celery seeds (to taste)

Preheat oven to 350°. On each of four square 9 inch pieces of aluminum foil, place a fish fillet and a portion of potatoes, carrots, and onions. Add 1 tablespoon butter to each square. Sprinkle with seasonings.

Fold foil over and seal edges well. Bake on a cookie sheet for 45 minutes. This can also be put on the grill. Serves 4.

Fish Patties With Salsa

1   pound fish, cooked and flaked
½   cup onion, chopped finely, or 1 tsp. onion powder
2   Tbsp. lemon juice
1   tsp. fresh or ½ tsp. dried marjoram
½   tsp. salt
½   tsp. dry mustard
2   slices dairy free bread, made into bread crumbs
2   eggs, beaten
1   Tbsp. vegetable oil
     salsa

Mix all the ingredients except the oil and salsa. Shape into 8 patties. Heat oil in a skillet over medium heat. Add patties and cook about 8 minutes, until golden brown. Serve with salsa. Serves 2.

Notes

Desserts

Gluten Free Dairy Free Baking Tips

General Rules:

Shortening can be used in place of butter or margarine for most baking. You can also use dairy free butter but it is more expensive. If you want to try other oils, like coconut oil, you will just have to try each recipe and see how it works.

Gluten free all purpose flour comes in many varieties. The most common is a rice flour base. YOU MUST spoon the flour into your measuring cup and then level. DO NOT, I REPEAT DO NOT scoop it out of the bag. You will get too much flour and then your baking will be heavy and not light and fluffy.

Xanthan gum is a popular food additive that's commonly added to foods as a thickener or stabilizer. It makes it a great thickening, suspending and stabilizing agent for many products.

Gluten free all purpose flour comes with or without xanthan gum (or guar gum). If it is WITHOUT then you will need to add xanthan gum to help the recipe stay together and be fluffier.

Mix Well! When baking breads and cookies with gluten free all purpose flour you want to make sure that you THOROUGHLY mix the batter. For gluten free bread that will mean 3-5 minutes mixing with the mixer.

Longer Baking Time - A lot of gluten free baking will take a few minutes longer to bake. I've adjusted the time so the recipes are correct in this cookbook but if you are trying to turn "regular" recipes into gluten free, you may need to bake longer.

Milk - You can use almost any dairy free milk for dairy free baking. The different milks will bring different flavors to your baking. As a general rule, rice milk and soy milk have the most neutral flavor for baking.

Cake, Frosting And Filling Tips

To frost a cake:

Brush loose crumbs from the sides of the cake and spread on a thin base coat of frosting.

Dip your knife into water from time to time to spread frosting easily. Let the cake set. Then apply a finishing coat.

If you want a flat cake, cut the rounded top off, turn it over and use the flat side as the top.

Place 2 pieces of waxed paper under the cake. Frost. Then gently pull the waxed paper out from under the cake. Your cake plate will stay clean!

- **Dust cakes with powdered sugar.** Place a doily on top of the cake. Sprinkle with powdered sugar. Then gently lift the doily off.

- **When a cake recipe calls for flouring the baking pan,** use a bit of the dry cake mix instead. This eliminates white mess on the outside of the cake.

- **Use cake or brownie crumbs** for ice cream topping.

- **Put gluten free all purpose flour in an old spice bottle** to dust pans for cakes.

- **When cooking in glass pans,** reduce the temperature by 25°.

- **To prevent dried fruits and nuts from sinking to the bottom** of a dessert or cake, mix with gluten free flour before adding to the batter.

Applesauce Cake

½	cup shortening
1½	cups sugar
2	eggs, beaten
½	tsp. salt
1	tsp. cinnamon
½	tsp. cloves
1	tsp. xanthan gum (if not in flour)
2½	cups gluten free all purpose flour
1½	cups applesauce
1	tsp. baking soda in 2 Tbsp. hot water
1	cup raisins
½	cup nuts (optional)

Preheat oven to 350°. Cream together shortening and sugar until fluffy.

Add eggs, salt, cinnamon, cloves and xanthan gum (if using). Mix well. Add flour and applesauce alternately.

Dissolve baking soda in hot water and pour into mixture. Stir. Fold in raisins and nuts. Bake in a greased 9x13 inch pan for 45 minutes.

- **When you have a partially eaten apple, save the good part and chop into pieces. Place in a microwave safe dish. Blend together 1 teaspoon each brown sugar, gluten free all purpose flour, oatmeal, dairy free butter and a dash of cinnamon. Place mixture over apple and microwave until apple is tender.**

- **To soften marshmallows that have become hard, place them in a resealable plastic bag with a few slices of fresh bread for a few days. To prevent drying out, store in your freezer.**

Apple Cake

2   cups sugar
1   tsp. salt
1   tsp. baking soda
1   Tbsp. baking powder
2½ cups gluten free all purpose flour
1   tsp. xanthan gum (if not in flour)
1¼ cups vegetable oil
2   eggs
3   cups apples, chopped
1   cup nuts (optional)

Preheat oven to 350°. Place all ingredients in a mixing bowl and mix well. Pour into a greased 9x13 inch baking pan and bake 1 hour, until a knife inserted in the middle comes out clean.

> Not only did I fall off the diet wagon
> but I dragged it into the woods,
> set it on fire and used the
> insurance money to buy cupcakes.

Banana Cake

½ cup shortening
¾ cup brown sugar, packed
½ cup sugar
2 eggs
1 cup ripe bananas, (2-3 medium), mashed
½ tsp. vinegar
1 tsp. vanilla
2 cups gluten free all purpose flour
1 tsp. xanthan gum (if not in flour)
1 tsp. baking soda
1 tsp. salt
½ cup dairy free milk (rice or soy)
½ cup nuts, chopped (optional)

Preheat oven to 350°. In a bowl, cream shortening and sugars. Add eggs, one at a time, beating well after each addition. Beat in bananas, vinegar and vanilla.

Combine flour, xanthan gum (if using), baking soda and salt. Add to creamed mixture alternately with milk. Stir in nuts. Pour into a greased 9x13 inch pan.

Bake 25-30 minutes or until a toothpick put in the center of the cake comes out clean. Cool and frost with Caramel Frosting (p.236). Serves 18.

> If you fatten up
> everyone else around you,
> you will look thinner.

Hot Fudge Lava Cake

1   cup gluten free all purpose flour
½   tsp. xanthan gum (if not in flour)
¾   cup sugar
2   Tbsp. cocoa
2   tsp. baking powder
¼   tsp. salt
½   cup dairy free milk (rice or soy)
2   Tbsp. shortening or dairy free butter, melted
1   tsp. vanilla
½   cup nuts

Topping

3   Tbsp. cocoa
½   cup sugar
1   cup hot water

Preheat oven to 350°. Mix all the ingredients and pour into a deep casserole dish buttered with dairy free butter.

For topping, mix cocoa and sugar and sprinkle on top of batter. Pour hot water over the top and bake 35-40 minutes. This has a delicious fudge sauce in the center when baked. Serves 9.

· **To make cupcakes all the same size, use an ice cream scoop to measure the batter.**

Elly's One Minute Chocolate Cake

4   Tbsp. gluten free all purpose flour
3   Tbsp. sugar
½   tsp. baking powder
⅛   tsp. salt
2   Tbsp. cocoa powder
½   tsp. vanilla
2   Tbsp. vegetable oil*
4   Tbsp. water
1   Tbsp. dairy free chocolate chips
    pinch xanthan gum (if not in flour)

Combine dry ingredients and mix very well. Add the liquids and chocolate chips and stir. Then transfer to a little dish, ramekin or coffee mug. Microwave 70 seconds. Enjoy!

I want someone to look at me

the way I look at chocolate cake...

Red Velvet Cake

¾ cup butter flavored shortening or dairy free butter
1 Tbsp. vinegar
2 eggs
1½ cups sugar
1½ tsp. cocoa
¼ tsp. salt
1 tsp. baking soda
2 tsp. vanilla
1-2 oz. red food coloring
1 tsp. xanthan gum (if not in flour)
2½ cups gluten free all purpose flour
1 cup dairy free milk (rice or soy)

Preheat oven to 350°. Cream together butter, vinegar, eggs and sugar in a bowl. Add the rest of the ingredients except the flour and milk. Mix well. Add flour and milk alternately. Beat until all the lumps are out.

Pour into a greased 9x13 inch pan floured with gluten free flour. Bake 30 minutes or until a toothpick inserted in the center comes out clean. Frost with Red Velvet Frosting. Serves 18.

Red Velvet Frosting

⅔ cup dairy free milk (rice or soy)
½ cup gluten free all purpose flour
½ cup dairy free butter
½ cup sugar
1 tsp. vanilla

In a saucepan, heat milk and flour until thick, stirring constantly. Cool thoroughly.

Beat milk and flour for 1 minute until fluffy. In a bowl, beat butter and sugar until creamy. Add to milk and flour. Then add vanilla. Mix well. Frosts 1 Red Velvet Cake.

Pound Cake

Tastes even better the next day!

2¾ cups sugar
1¼ cups butter flavored shortening or dairy free butter, softened
1   tsp. vanilla
5   eggs
3   cups gluten free all purpose flour
1½ tsp. xanthan gum (if not in flour)
1   tsp. baking powder
¼   tsp. salt
1   cup dairy free milk (rice or soy)

Preheat oven to 350°. In a large bowl, combine sugar, butter, vanilla and eggs. Beat on low until mixed, about 1 minute, scraping bowl constantly.

Beat on high speed for 5 minutes, occasionally scraping the bowl.

Mix flour, xanthan gum (if using), baking powder and salt. Beat into egg mixture alternately with milk on low speed. Spread in a well-greased 10x4 inch tube pan.

Bake 70 to 80 minutes or until a toothpick inserted in the center comes out clean. Cool 20 minutes in the pan. Then remove onto a wire rack and cool completely. Serves 8-10.

- **To cut a layer cake in half horizontally to frost or fill, use a length of dental floss or sewing thread. Just wrap the thread around the sides of the cake, making sure it is centered and even. Cross the ends of the thread over each other and pull gently to slice the cake into two layers. The floss makes a neater cut.**

- **To chop nuts, place them in a plastic bag and roll them with a rolling pin.**

- **To send a piece of frosted cake in a lunch pail, slice the cake in half horizontally and then make a "sandwich" with the frosting in the middle. It won't stick to the plastic wrap.**

Spice Cake

1	cup butter flavored shortening or dairy free butter
2¼	cups sugar
5	eggs
3	cups gluten free all purpose flour
1½	tsp. xanthan gum (if not in flour)
1	Tbsp. ground cloves
1	Tbsp. cinnamon
	pinch of salt
1	cup dairy free milk (rice or soy)
1	tsp. vinegar
1	tsp. baking soda
	powdered sugar

Preheat oven to 350°. Cream shortening until soft. Gradually add sugar until mixture is very light and fluffy.

In a separate bowl, beat the eggs thoroughly and add to creamed mixture. Mix well.

Mix flour, xanthan gum (if using), cloves, cinnamon and salt. Beat about ⅓ of the flour combination into the batter. Then stir in half the milk and the vinegar.

Add another third of the flour-spice combination and mix thoroughly. Stir baking soda into the remaining ½ cup of milk and mix into batter, along with the remaining flour.

Pour into a greased 10 inch tube pan. Bake 55-65 minutes or until a toothpick inserted in the center of the cake comes out clean. Cool 10 minutes before removing from pan.

When cool, sprinkle or sift powdered sugar over the top, or frost with Caramel Frosting (p.236). Serves 15.

- **To keep your place in a recipe, place all ingredients on the right side of the bowl. As they are used, move them to the left side.**

What Cake

1   cup gluten free oatmeal
½   cup butter flavored shortening or dairy free butter
1½   cups boiling water
1   tsp. baking soda
1½   tsp. cinnamon
½   tsp. salt
1½   cup gluten free all purpose flour
½   tsp. xanthan gum (if not in flour)
1   cup plus 2 Tbsp. sugar
1   cup brown sugar, packed
2   eggs, beaten

Preheat oven to 375°. Mix oatmeal and shortening together. Pour boiling water over them to soften. Add remaining ingredients. Mix well and pour into a greased 9x13 inch pan.

Bake 30-40 minutes. Spread topping over cake. Serves 18.

Topping

¾   cup brown sugar
2   Tbsp. dairy free milk (rice or soy)
6   Tbsp. dairy free butter
1   cup coconut
     nuts (optional)

Combine brown sugar, milk and butter in a saucepan and bring to a boil. Boil for 1 minute. Add coconut and nuts and stir. Spread onto cake. Put under broiler until lightly browned.

White Cake

4	eggs
2	cups sugar
2½	cups gluten free all purpose flour
½	tsp. salt
1	Tbsp. baking powder
1	tsp. xanthan gum (if not in flour)
1	cup dairy free milk (rice or soy)
1	tsp. vinegar
1	cup shortening, melted and cooled
2	tsp. vanilla

Preheat oven to 350°. Grease (2) 8 inch round cake pans and line the bottom of each pan with a greased parchment circle.

Beat eggs and sugar until creamy. Add dry ingredients and mix well. Add milk, vinegar, shortening and vanilla and beat to combine.

Divide batter between pans. Bake in center of oven for 35-40 minutes, until the cake is very lightly browned and a toothpick inserted in the center comes out clean. Remove and let cool **at least 30 minutes**, before inverting onto a wire rack to finish cooling. Frost as desired.

Bake for the times listed below:

8 inch pan	35-40 minutes
9 inch pan	35-40 minutes
9x13 inch	40-45 minutes
30 cupcakes	18- 20 minutes

Yellow Cake

¾   cup butter flavored shortening or dairy free butter, softened
1½ cups sugar
2½ tsp. vanilla
3   eggs
1⅓ cups dairy free milk (rice or soy)
1   tsp. vinegar
½   tsp. salt
3   cups gluten free all purpose flour
1   tsp. xanthan gum (if not in flour)
3   tsp. baking powder

Preheat oven to 350°. Beat shortening and sugar together in a bowl until fluffy. Add vanilla and eggs one at a time, beating well after each addition, scraping the sides constantly. Add milk and vinegar and beat well.

Add dry ingredients and mix well.

Pour into 1 well greased 9x13 inch pan floured with gluten free flour or three 8-inch or two 9 inch pans. Serves 18.

Bake for the times listed below:

8 inch pan	23-28 minutes
9 inch pan	30-35 minutes
9x13 inch	40-45 minutes
30 cupcakes	20-25 minutes

Cake is done when a toothpick inserted into the center comes out clean. Cool completely. Frost with chocolate frosting (p.237).

•   **For better accuracy when decorating a picture on a cake, take a cookie cutter and put an imprint on the top of the cake. Then follow the lines as you are piping the frosting on the cake.**

Chocolate Cake

½	cup + 1 Tbsp. butter flavored shortening or dairy free butter, softened
2	cups sugar
2	eggs, room temperature
1	tsp. vanilla
2	cups gluten free all purpose flour
1	tsp. xanthan gum (if not in flour)
1	tsp. baking soda
½	tsp. baking powder
1	tsp. salt
¾	cup cocoa powder
1	cup dairy free milk (rice or soy) with 1 Tbsp. vinegar added
¾	cup boiling water

Preheat oven to 350°. Line two 8 inch baking pans with parchment paper and spray with cooking spray.

In a large bowl, cream butter and sugar with a mixer. Add eggs and vanilla to butter mixture and mix until fully combined. Add flour, xanthan gum (if using), baking soda, baking powder, salt and cocoa powder. Mix until fully combined, scraping down sides as needed.

Add the milk and mix until fully combined.

Add the boiling water to the batter and mix until fully combined.

Pour half of the batter into each pan.

Bake on the middle rack for 30-35 minutes.

Check the center of the cake by inserting a toothpick or knife to make sure it is done. You will also see the sides of the cake pulling away from the side of the pan.

Allow the cakes to cool fully before frosting.

Zucchini Cake

2   cups gluten free all purpose flour
1   tsp. xanthan gum (if not in flour)
2   cups zucchini, grated
1¼ cups sugar
½   cup vegetable oil
⅓   cup water
1¼ tsp. baking soda
1   tsp. salt
1   tsp. cinnamon
1   tsp. cloves
1   tsp. nutmeg
1   tsp. vanilla
3   eggs
1   tsp. vinegar

Preheat oven to 350°. Mix all the ingredients in a bowl and beat on low for 1 minute, scraping bowl constantly. Beat on medium for 2 minutes, scraping bowl occasionally. Pour into a greased 9x13 inch pan. Bake for about 45 minutes. Serves 18.

It would be easier to lose weight

if replacement parts

weren't so handy in the

refrigerator.

Baker's Frosting

1   lb. (4 cups) powdered sugar
½   cup shortening
¼   tsp. salt
½   tsp. vanilla
4   Tbsp. water
     food coloring

Mix ingredients in a bowl and beat on high with a hand mixer for 10 minutes. Add food coloring, as desired. Use to decorate wedding and birthday cakes. Frosts one 9x13 inch cake.

Buttercream Frosting

3   cups powdered sugar
⅓   cup butter flavored shortening or dairy free butter, softened
1½ tsp. vanilla
1-2 Tbsp. dairy free milk (rice or soy)

Mix powdered sugar and shortening or butter. Stir in vanilla and 1 tablespoon milk. Beat until smooth. If the frosting is too stiff, add 1 more tablespoon of milk and beat again until smooth. Frosts one 9x13 inch cake or two 8 inch cakes. This can easily be halved. Frosting can also be refrigerated several weeks.

Peppermint Frosting

Use peppermint flavoring instead of vanilla.

Caramel Frosting

½   cup dairy free butter
1   cup brown sugar, packed
¼   cup dairy free milk (rice or soy)
2   cups powdered sugar

Heat butter over medium heat in a 2 quart saucepan. When butter is melted, stir in brown sugar. Heat to boiling, stirring constantly.

Reduce heat to low and boil 2 minutes longer, still stirring. Stir in milk and heat to boiling. Remove from heat and cool. Slowly stir in powdered sugar.

Place saucepan of frosting in a bowl of very cold water and beat frosting until smooth. If frosting is too stiff, add an additional 1 teaspoon of milk at a time until the frosting is smooth.

Frosts one 9x13 inch cake.

Dear Diet,

Things are just not going to work out for us.
It is not me it is you. You are tasteless, boring
and I can't stop cheating on you.

Chocolate Frosting

¼   cup dairy free butter, melted
¼   tsp. salt
½   cup cocoa
¼   cup dairy free milk (rice or soy)
1½   tsp. vanilla
3½   cup powdered sugar

Put all the ingredients in a bowl and beat until smooth. Frosts one 9x13 inch cake.

Fluffy White Frosting

1½   cups sugar
2   egg whites
⅓   cup water
¼   tsp. cream of tartar
1   tsp. vanilla

In a saucepan over low heat, combine sugar, egg whites, water and cream of tartar. With a hand mixer, beat mixture on low for 1 minute.

Continue to beat on low speed over low heat until frosting reaches 160° (about 8-10 minutes).

Pour into a large mixing bowl and add vanilla. Beat on high until frosting forms stiff peaks (about 7 minutes). Makes 7 cups.

Vanilla Glaze

⅓ cup dairy free butter
2 cups powdered sugar
1½ tsp. vanilla
2-4 Tbsp. hot water

Heat butter in a saucepan until melted. Stir in powdered sugar,
vanilla and 1 tablespoon water. Mix well. Add the rest of the water, 1
tablespoon at a time, until the frosting is smooth. Glazes one bundt
cake or one 10 inch angel food cake.

Lemon Glaze

Starting with the Vanilla Glaze recipe, substitute 1⅓ tsp. lemon juice
for the vanilla and add ½ tsp. grated lemon peel to the butter.

Cupcake Filling

5 Tbsp. gluten free all purpose flour
1 cup dairy free milk (rice or soy)
½ cup dairy free butter
½ cup shortening
¾ cup sugar
1 tsp. vanilla

Mix flour and milk in saucepan. Cook on medium heat, stirring
constantly until a paste forms. Cool. In a bowl, cream together butter,
shortening, sugar and vanilla. Beat 5 minutes. Add flour paste and
mix 5 more minutes. With a long pastry tip, poke a hole in the center
of each cupcake and fill. Fills one cupcake recipe or makes a good
center filling for layer cakes. Fills 20-24 cupcakes.

Pie Tips

- **For Pies:** Berry pies can be frozen unbaked.

- Freeze pumpkin puree for pies in 2 cup portions.

- For an extra treat: **Place leftover pieces of rolled out pie crust** on a baking sheet. Sprinkle with cinnamon and sugar. Bake 10-15 minutes at 425° while baking pies.

- **Use leftover pie crust** to make one or two pocket sandwiches or a couple of mini pot pies.

- **If you have trouble learning to make pies,** make 10 pies in a row during 1 week. Practice makes perfect. Even if you have a couple of failures with the first few pies, in the long run it will save you money.

- **Brush beaten egg white over pie crust** before baking. This will give your pie crust a beautiful glossy finish.

- **Substitute gluten free oatmeal,** browned in a bit of dairy free butter, for nuts in cookies, cakes, and pies. The oatmeal adds a nice flavor and crunch.

- **If you don't have enough dough to make a top crust,** simply use a lattice top instead.

Ohhh, Pilates -
I thought you said Pie and Lattes.

Pie Crust

The BEST Dairy Free Gluten Free Pie Crust Ever!

2	cups gluten free all purpose flour
	(tested with Pamela's gluten free all purpose flour)
1	tsp. xanthan gum (if not in flour)
½	tsp. salt
1	Tbsp. sugar
½	cup butter flavored shortening, cold
	(regular shortening can be used)
1	egg, cold
1	Tbsp. vinegar, cold
⅔	cup water, cold
	sugar

Mix flour, xanthan gum (if using), salt and sugar in a bowl. Cut in shortening with a pastry blender or 2 knives (I use my fingers). Add egg, vinegar and 3 tablespoons water. Mix lightly. If dough is too dry, add more water. Mix with hands. Don't over mix. Mix just until the dough sticks together.

Divide in half. Roll out to make 2 pies crusts. When using the crust for the top of the pie, sprinkle sugar on top and poke crust to make a few steam holes. The crust can be frozen in balls and then defrosted and rolled out when ready to use. Makes 2 crusts.

Baked Pie Crust: Preheat oven to 425° with a rack in the lower middle position. Roll out the pie crust and transfer to the pie plate as normal. Line top of crust with parchment paper or aluminum foil.

Fill with beans or pie weights. Make sure they cover the bottom of the pie and press against the sides of the pie. This keeps the pie crust from puffing up or sagging as the crust bakes.

Place the pie on the baking sheet and bake until the edges of the crust just start to turn golden, 12 to 15 minutes.

Grasp corners of the parchment (or foil) and lift weights out of the pie. The bottom of the pie will still look wet and un-cooked at this point.

Return the crust to the oven. Bake until the bottom looks dry, another 5 minutes. If the pie will not be cooked again with the filling, bake for another few minutes until the edges of the crust have browned and the bottom is lightly golden. The bottom crust will puff a bit as it bakes, but will deflate again when you remove the pie from the oven. Fill pie with pie filling and bake as directed.

Graham Cracker Crust

2   cups gluten free graham cracker crumbs
3   Tbsp. sugar
½   cup dairy free butter, melted

Preheat oven to 350°. Mix all ingredients together and press into a 9 inch pie plate.

Bake 10 minutes. Cool and fill with your favorite pudding filling. Makes 1 crust.

Grandma's Apple Pie

6-7   cups medium apples, cored, peeled and thinly sliced
½   cup sugar
¼   cup brown sugar
¼   tsp. salt
¾   tsp. cinnamon
¼   tsp. nutmeg
2   Tbsp. cornstarch
2   pie crusts (p.240)
2   Tbsp. dairy free butter

Preheat oven to 450°. Mix all ingredients in a large bowl, except the butter and crust. Microwave this filling mixture 2-3 minutes. Then pour into the pie crust.

Dot with butter and top with the other crust. Cut steam slits in the top crust and sprinkle the top with sugar.

Bake 15 minutes. Then turn down to 350° and bake for 35-45 more minutes, until apples are tender and juices are bubbling nicely out of the steam slits.

Cherry Pie

1¼ cups sugar
2½ Tbsp. cornstarch
¼   tsp. salt
1   qt. tart red cherries, pitted
2   pie crusts (p.240)
2   Tbsp. dairy free butter

Preheat oven to 425°. Mix sugar, cornstarch, salt and cherries together. Line pie pan with pie crust. Add cherry mixture. Dot with butter and cover with top crust. Bake 10 minutes. Then reduce heat to 350° and bake 25 minutes longer. Makes one pie.

Peach Pie

2   pie crusts (p.240)
⅔   cup sugar
3   Tbsp. cornstarch
¼   tsp. cinnamon
6   cups sliced peaches (fresh, frozen or canned, drained)
1   tsp. lemon juice
2   Tbsp. dairy free butter

Preheat oven to 425°. Prepare pie crust. Mix the rest of the ingredients in a large bowl.

Place pie crust in a 9 inch pie plate. Add peach mixture and dot with dairy free butter. Cover with top crust and cut a few slits in it. (I cut my initial in the top.) Seal and flute the edges. Cover edges with a 2 inch strip of aluminum foil to prevent them from burning.

Bake 30 minutes. Remove foil and continue to bake for an additional 15 minutes. Remove from oven and cool slightly before serving. Makes one pie.

Pecan Pie

½   cup dairy free butter
1   cup light corn syrup
1   cup sugar
3   large eggs
½   tsp. lemon juice
1   tsp. vanilla
     dash of salt
1¼ cups pecans, chopped
1   pie crust (p.240)

Preheat oven to 425°. In a medium microwave safe bowl, melt butter and cool. When cooled, add the other ingredients into the butter in the order given and mix well. Pour into pie crust. Bake 10 minutes at 425° and then 40 minutes at 325°. Makes one pie.

Pumpkin Pie

1   pie crust, unbaked (p.240)
2   eggs
1   (15 oz.) can pumpkin
¾   cup sugar
½   tsp. salt
1   tsp. cinnamon
½   tsp. ginger
¼   tsp. cloves
1½ cups dairy free milk (rice or soy)

Preheat oven to 350°. Bake pie crust for 1-2 minutes until crust starts to puff with small bubbles. Watch carefully. Remove from oven.

Turn oven up to 425°. Blend all remaining ingredients together in a bowl. Pour into pie crust and bake for 15 minutes.

Then turn the oven down to 350° and bake for 45 more minutes. The pie is done when a knife inserted into the center comes out clean. Makes one pie.

Strawberry Pie

1½   cups sugar
1½   cups water
3   Tbsp. cornstarch
6   oz. strawberry gelatin
1½-2 cups fresh strawberries
1   baked pie crust (p.240)
      coconut whipped cream

Mix sugar, water and cornstarch in a saucepan. Cook until thick and clear. Remove from the heat and add gelatin. Mix well. Place strawberries in a pie crust and pour sugar/gelatin mix over them. Chill. Top with whipped cream and garnish with more strawberries.

Chocolate Pie

1½   cups sugar
⅓   cup cornstarch
½   tsp. salt
⅓   cup cocoa
3   cups dairy free milk (coconut)
4   egg yolks
2   Tbsp. dairy free butter
2   tsp. vanilla
1   9-inch, baked pie crust (p.240)
      coconut whipped cream

In a saucepan, combine sugar, cornstarch, salt and cocoa. Blend milk and egg yolks and add to cornstarch mixture. Cook over medium heat to boiling, stirring constantly. Boil 1 minute.

Add butter and vanilla. Pour into baked pie crust. Chill. Top with coconut whipped cream. Makes one pie.

Coconut Pie

1½ cups dairy free milk (coconut)
¼ cup sugar
¼ tsp. salt
3 Tbsp. cornstarch
1 egg yolk
1 Tbsp. dairy free butter
½ tsp. vanilla
1½ cups coconut
1 baked pie crust (p.240)
  coconut whipped cream

In a medium saucepan over medium heat, mix milk, sugar, salt and cornstarch. Stir. Cook slowly until thickened, stirring constantly.

Whisk egg yolk in a medium mixing bowl. Add cornstarch mixture slowly to egg yolk in bowl. Pour back into saucepan and cook 1 minute longer.

Add butter and vanilla. Stir in coconut. Cool. Pour into baked pie crust and chill. Top with whipped cream if desired. Makes one pie.

Banana Pie

Substitute 4 sliced ripe bananas for coconut. Alternate layers of bananas and cooled filling.

Lemon Meringue Pie

5   Tbsp. cornstarch
1½   cups sugar
½   tsp. salt
2   cups boiling water
3   egg yolks (save whites for meringue)
4   Tbsp. lemon juice
2   Tbsp. dairy free butter
2   Tbsp. grated lemon rind
1   pie crust (p.240), baked

Combine dry ingredients. Add water. Cook until thick, stirring constantly. Place egg yolks in a small bowl. Beat slightly.

Add ¼ cup of hot cornstarch mixture 1 tablespoon at a time, mixing after each addition to the eggs. (This keeps the eggs from scrambling when added to the saucepan.)

Add egg mixture to the saucepan. Simmer 2 minutes, stirring occasionally. Add the rest of the ingredients. Stir until mixed. Pour into pie crust. Cover with meringue. Makes one 9 inch pie.

Meringue

1   Tbsp. cornstarch
½   Tbsp. cold water
½   cup boiling water
3   egg whites
6   Tbsp. sugar
1   tsp. vanilla

In a saucepan, mix cornstarch with cold water. Add boiling water and cook until thick on medium heat. Set aside to cool. Beat egg whites to soft peaks. Add cornstarch mixture and beat until stiff. Add sugar, 1 tablespoon at a time, until all is incorporated. Then add vanilla. Cover the top of the pie with Meringue. Bake at 325° for 15 minutes. Turn off oven, leave pie in oven and let cool with door open. DO NOT cut until completely cooled.

Pineapple Millionaire Pie

2   cups powdered sugar
½   cup dairy free butter
2   large eggs (pasteurized eggs may be used)
⅛   tsp. salt
¼   tsp. vanilla
1   pie crust (p.240)

Cream ingredients and pour into a baked pie crust. Chill 1 hour.

¼   cup powdered sugar
1   cup crushed pineapple (drained)
½   cup pecans
2   cups coconut whipped cream (p.310)

Mix first three ingredients. Fold in whipped topping. Spread onto chilled base mixture. Chill well before serving. Makes one 9 inch pie.

I exercised once and found out

I was allergic to it.

My skin flushed, my heart raced,

I got sweaty and short of breath.

Very dangerous.

Candy Tips

- Be very careful when making homemade candies. If you don't get **everything on sale** for a really good price then it can be more expensive than buying the candy pre-made.

- Use the **leftover syrup from candied orange peels** on pancakes, waffles or French toast for a gourmet taste.

- If you **overcook chocolate**, it becomes dull looking. To save it, put the pan on low heat and beat in 1 teaspoon at a time shortening or oil until you have restored the shiny, smooth consistency.

- When you are **melting chocolate**, make sure that **all utensils are completely dry**. Even a little water will make chocolate grainy and lumpy.

Candy Cooking Tests

When placed in a cold cup of water, candy will:

Soft Ball	234°-240°	form a soft ball that can be flattened
Firm Ball	242°-248°	form a firm ball that holds its shape until pressed
Hard Ball	250°-268°	form a ball that is pliable and holds its shape
Soft Crack	270°-290°	separates into hard but not brittle threads
Hard Crack	300°-310°	cracks easily
Caramel	320°-350°	mixture coats metal spoon and forms light caramel colored mass when poured onto a plate
For High Altitude		lower candy temperature 2° for each 1,000 feet of elevation.

- **Check the accuracy of your thermometer by placing in boiling water. It should read 212° at sea level or 203° at 5000 feet.**

Applesauce Candy

1   cup applesauce*
1   cup sugar
1   pkg. fruit gelatin
½   cup nuts, finely chopped
     extra sugar for coating

Combine applesauce and sugar in a saucepan. Bring to a boil and cook 2 minutes. Dissolve the gelatin in the applesauce mixture. Add the nuts and pour into an 8x8 inch pan.

After 24 hours, cut into 1 inch squares and roll in sugar. Roll in the sugar a second time 24 hours later. Makes 64 pieces.

*Puree fruit cocktail, peaches or pears instead of applesauce.

If swimming is so good

for your figure,

then why do whales

look the way they do?

Candied Orange Peels

peels from 3 large oranges or grapefruits*
water
2   Tbsp. corn syrup
2¾ cups sugar, divided

Slice peels into ¼ inch wide strips. Place peels into a 3 quart saucepan (do not use an aluminum pan) and cover with water. Bring to a boil, reduce heat and simmer for 15 minutes.

Drain and set aside. Boil ¾ cup water, corn syrup and 2 cups of the sugar until sugar dissolves. Add peels. Simmer 40 minutes, stirring occasionally.

Remove peels with a slotted spoon. Place peels on a rack that is set over a baking pan. Drain for 5 minutes. Separate peels and drain for another hour.

Toss peels with remaining sugar in a plastic bag. Allow to air dry for 3 more hours. Then store in an airtight container. These keep one month or can be frozen. Makes 30-40 pieces.

*Clean peels well before peeling. To peel fruit, score the outside of the fruit into quarters. Remove peel from fruit.

You call is important to us.

Please enjoy this 45 minutes flute solo.

2 Ingredient Fudge

1   12 oz. (pkg.) dairy free chocolate chips
1   10 oz. can sweetened condensed coconut milk

Melt together. Put into a greased 8x8 inch pan. Chill several hours. Then cut into squares. Makes 16 pieces.

Caramels

2   cups brown sugar, packed
1   cup white corn syrup
1½   cups (11 oz.) full fat coconut milk
1   cup dairy free butter
½   tsp. salt
1   tsp. vanilla
1   cup walnuts or pecans (optional)

Combine sugar, corn syrup, coconut milk, butter and salt in a saucepan. Heat gradually to boiling, stirring constantly. Boil to 235° (225° high altitude). This can take between 20-40 minutes.

Add vanilla and nuts. Pour into an 8 inch pan that has been well buttered with dairy free butter. Cool several hours or overnight. Cut into small squares. Makes 64 pieces.

2 Ingredient Coconut Haystacks

12   oz. dairy free chocolate chips
3-4 cups shredded coconut

Melt chocolate. Add desired amount of coconut. Place by spoonfuls on waxed paper or Silpat on a cookie sheet. Place in the fridge to harden.

Chocolate Covered Pretzels

1   pkg. gluten free pretzels*
1   pkg. dairy free white, dark or milk chocolate

Melt chocolate in the top of a double boiler. Remove from heat when melted. Dip pretzels in to cover. Set on waxed paper until cool.

*Gluten free cookies like Oreos can be used instead of pretzels.

Turtles

72   pecan halves (about 4 oz.)
24   coconut caramels
4   oz. dairy free semi-sweet chocolate

Preheat oven to 300°. Cover baking sheet with foil, shiny side up, and grease. For each candy, place 3 pecan halves into a "Y" shape on the foil. Place 1 caramel on the center of each "Y". Bake just until candy is melted. If they look deformed after baking, reshape while the caramel is warm.

Heat chocolate over low heat, stirring constantly, just until melted. Spoon mixture over candies, leaving the ends uncovered. Refrigerate until firm (about 30 minutes). Makes about 24 turtles.

• **Leftover melted chocolate from making candies? Pour it into a small non-stick cake pan, smooth it into an even layer and refrigerate until hardened. Then "pop" it out onto a cutting board, chop it into small chunks and store it in the fridge to be used later in any recipe that calls for chocolate chips.**

Chocolate Covered Peanuts

1   cup dairy free chocolate chips
1   cup peanuts*

Place the chocolate chips in a microwave safe bowl and microwave on high 1 to 2 minutes, stirring halfway through cooking, until melted. Stir in the nuts or dried fruit (or a combination of both).

Drop the mixture by the teaspoonful onto a waxed paper lined baking sheet and refrigerate until firm. Store at a cool room temperature. Makes 15 candies.

* Walnuts, raisins or chopped dried apricots may be used instead.

Mounds

22   gluten free graham crackers, crushed
½   cup dairy free butter, melted
3   Tbsp. sugar
1   (14 oz.) can sweetened condensed coconut milk
12   oz. coconut
1   (12 oz.) pkg. dairy free chocolate chips

Preheat oven to 325°. Mix graham crackers, butter and sugar and spread evenly into a 9x13 inch cake pan. Bake 5 minutes and cool.

In a saucepan, heat sweetened condensed milk and coconut for 10 minutes. Do not scorch.

Spread on crust. Put chocolate chips on top. Place in oven until chocolate chips melt. Chill before serving.

Makes 18 pieces.

Peppermint Patties

2½ cups powdered sugar
1   egg white (meringue powder may be substituted)
2   Tbsp. dairy free butter, melted
4   small lids peppermint flavoring
1   (12 oz.) pkg. dairy free chocolate chips
¼   cup palm shortening or coconut oil

Mix powdered sugar, egg white or meringue, butter and peppermint flavoring. Make into small balls about the size of a quarter and then flatten on a cookie sheet. Put in the freezer.

Melt chocolate and palm shortening over a double boiler or in the microwave. When melted, take mints out of the freezer. Put a toothpick through the center of the mint and dip into chocolate. Put back on cookie sheet and let chocolate harden in the freezer.

If mints on the cookie sheet begin to soften and thaw, refreeze, because they are easier to dip.

Wrap each mint in a piece of 5x5 inch foil. Makes twenty 2 inch mints.

If you have melted chocolate
all over your hands,
you're eating it too slowly!

Peanut Butter Cups

½ cup dairy free butter
1 cup peanut butter
2 cups powdered sugar
1 tsp. vanilla
1 (12 oz.) pkg. dairy free chocolate chips
¼ cup paraffin, shaved

Cream butter, peanut butter, sugar and vanilla.

In a microwave safe dish, place chocolate chips and paraffin. Microwave until melted, stirring frequently.

Pour a small amount of melted chocolate in the bottom of paper holders. Put in the filling and pour more chocolate on top until filling is covered. Let chocolate harden before serving. Makes 2 dozen.

Peanut Butter Balls

Shape peanut butter mixture from Peanut Butter Cups into small 1½ inch balls. Dip peanut butter balls into chocolate and place on wax paper to harden.

If you can't eat all of your chocolate,

it will keep in the freezer.

But, if you can't eat all of your chocolate,

what's wrong with you?

Peanut Brittle

This is Tawra's favorite candy in the whole wide world!

¾   cup corn syrup
2   cups sugar
¾   cup hot water
2   cups raw peanuts
1   tsp. baking soda
1½ tsp. salt

Grease 2 jelly roll pans. In a saucepan, add corn syrup, sugar and water. Bring to a boil and cook to a hard ball stage at 260°.

Add peanuts and cook to hard crack at 290°.

Add baking soda and salt. Stir well, pour into pans and spread thin. Cool quickly.

I usually make this for Christmas and don't have room left in my refrigerator so I just set it outside in the snow for a few minutes until it has cooled. Makes 3-4 dozen pieces.

Sugared Peanuts

1   cup sugar
½   cup water
2   cups raw peanuts, shelled

Preheat oven to 300°.

In a saucepan over medium heat, dissolve the sugar in water. Add nuts and continue to cook, stirring frequently. Cook until the nuts are coated and the bottom of the pan is dry (but not too dry).

Pour and spread over an ungreased cookie sheet. Bake about 30 minutes. Stir every 5 minutes.

Honey Roasted Nuts

3	cups nuts
2	Tbsp. dairy free butter
½	tsp. cinnamon
½	cup honey
½	tsp. orange peel, grated
	salt

Microwave all ingredients in bowl 4 to 7 minutes at high power, stirring halfway through cooking time. Spread nuts on foil to cool. Lightly salt. Makes 3 cups.

Sugared Nuts

3	cups walnut halves
1½	cups pecan halves
2	cups sugar
1	cup water
¼	tsp. cinnamon

Mix ingredients in a heavy skillet. Cook until water disappears and nuts have a sugary appearance. Remove from heat and pour nuts onto a baking sheet. Separate quickly with 2 forks. Makes 5 cups.

Vinegar Candy

2	cups sugar
½	cup cider vinegar
2	tsp. dairy free butter

Combine ingredients in a saucepan and cook to 275°. Pour into well buttered jelly roll pan, let cool, and break. Makes 24 pieces.

Marshmallow Bonbons

38-40 large marshmallows
     coconut (optional)
     sprinkles (optional)
     nuts, chopped (optional)
1   (12 oz.) pkg. dairy free chocolate chips

Place marshmallows on a pan that is covered with wax paper and place in the freezer. They will be ready by the time you need to dip them.

Pour coconut, sprinkles and nuts on squares of wax paper. You could use a bowl, but wax paper saves time and effort in clean up.

Melt the chocolate chips in the microwave for a couple of minutes, stirring every 30 seconds, until melted.

Place frozen marshmallows on a skewer or toothpick and dip in chocolate. Then roll in coconut, sprinkles and nuts or your choice of toppings (below).

Use a fork to slide them back on the wax paper. Chill. Once chilled, you can package in clear cellophane bags.

Recommended Toppings

- Coconut, toasted
- Sprinkles
- Nuts, crushed
- Gluten free graham cracker crumbs (like s'mores)
- Peppermint sticks, crushed
- Candy, crushed
- Dried fruit, chopped
- Sweetened cereal, crushed

Snickerdoodles

1 cup butter flavored shortening or dairy free butter
2 eggs
2¾ cup gluten free all purpose flour
1 tsp. xanthan gum (if not in flour)
½ tsp. salt
1 tsp. baking soda
2 tsp. cream of tartar
1½ cups sugar
2 Tbsp. sugar
2 tsp. cinnamon

Preheat oven to 400°. In a large bowl, cream shortening until light.

Add eggs and beat until smooth.

Add flour, xanthan gum (if using), salt, baking soda, cream of tartar and 1½ cups sugar. Mix on low until combined.

Mix remaining cinnamon and sugar.

Shape dough into small balls. Roll in cinnamon and sugar. Place on an ungreased baking sheet 2 inches apart.

Bake for 8-10 minutes until light brown. Cool 5-10 minutes on cookie sheet then move to racks.

No Bake Fudge Cookies

½   cup dairy free milk (rice or soy)
2   cups sugar
½   cup baking cocoa
½   cup dairy free butter
½   cup nuts (optional)
½   cup peanut butter (smooth or chunky) (optional)
1   tsp. vanilla
3   cups gluten free oatmeal

Mix milk, sugar, cocoa and butter in a saucepan. Bring to a rolling boil and boil 1 minute. Remove from heat. Add nuts, peanut butter and vanilla and stir well. Add oatmeal and mix until well coated.

Drop by teaspoonfuls onto waxed paper and let cool until hardened.

If the humidity is very high or if you didn't let them boil long enough they won't set. If this happens, scoop the cookies off the wax paper and store to use as an ice cream topping. Makes 2 dozen.

The parenting skill I am most proud of is shoving a whole candy bar in my mouth and talking normally around it when a kid walks in.

Chocolate Cookies

1¼ cups butter flavored shortening or dairy free butter, softened
2   cups sugar
2   eggs
2   tsp. vanilla
2   cups gluten free all purpose flour
1   tsp. xanthan gum (if not in flour)
¾   cup cocoa, packed
1   tsp. baking soda
½   tsp. salt

Preheat oven to 350°. Cream shortening or butter, sugar and eggs. Add vanilla. Combine flour, xanthan gum (if using), cocoa, baking soda and salt. Add to creamed mixture. Drop by teaspoonfuls onto a cookie sheet and bake 8-9 minutes. Cool.

GF DF Oreos

Spread Buttercream Frosting (p.235) between cookies to make sandwiches. Makes 1 dozen.

Ice Cream Sandwiches

Slice a frozen brick of ice cream into 1 inch slices. Use a biscuit cutter about the same size as your cookies and cut rounds out of the ice cream. Place in between 2 cookies. Wrap in plastic wrap and store frozen.

Ginger Creams

¼ cup shortening
½ cup sugar
1 egg
½ cup molasses
2 cups gluten free all purpose flour
1 tsp. xanthan gum (if not in flour)
½ tsp. salt
1 tsp. ginger
½ tsp. nutmeg
½ tsp. cloves
½ tsp. cinnamon
1 tsp. baking soda dissolved in ¼ cup hot water

Preheat oven to 400°.

Mix all ingredients. Drop by teaspoonfuls and place on a greased cookie sheet. Bake until brown, about 5-10 minutes.

Cool and frost with Buttercream Frosting (p.235), if desired. Makes 3 dozen.

I like to make lists,
then leave them on the kitchen table
and then guess what is on the list
while I am at the store.

Ginger Spice Snaps

1	cup brown sugar, packed
¾	cup shortening
1	egg
¼	cup honey or dark corn syrup
1	tsp. ginger
½	tsp. salt
½	tsp. cinnamon
¼	tsp. cloves
1½	tsp. baking soda
2¼	cups gluten free all purpose flour
1	tsp. xanthan gum (if not in flour)

Preheat oven to 350°. In a mixing bowl, cream brown sugar and shortening. Add the egg and honey or corn syrup and mix well.

Add all the dry ingredients and stir into the sugar mixture until well blended.

Shape into balls. Dip half the ball in water, then in sugar. Place sugar side up.

Bake on an ungreased cookie sheet for 12-15 minutes. Let cool COMPLETELY before removing from cookie sheet. Makes 2 dozen.

- **When using a recipe card, slip the card between the tines of a fork and stand the fork in a glass. The card will be held at just the right angle for reading and will be safe from spills.**

Mudslide Cookies

2¾ cups powdered sugar
¾ cup cocoa powder
¼ tsp. salt
3 egg whites (room temperature)
1 Tbsp. vanilla
¾ cup dairy free semi-sweet chocolate chips
½ cup dairy free dark chocolate chips
½ coconut, shredded (optional)

Preheat oven to 350°. Line two cookie sheets with parchment paper. Spray top of parchment paper with nonstick cooking spray.

In a bowl, add the powdered sugar, cocoa powder and salt. Mix together. Add the egg whites and vanilla and mix on low until mixed. Batter will be very thick when done!

Stir in the semi-sweet chips, dark chocolate chips and coconut, if desired.

Using a medium cookie scoop, scoop out wet dough mounds onto cookie sheet, leaving plenty of room for them to spread during baking.

Bake one sheet at a time for even baking. If you need to use the same cookie sheet twice, be sure to let it cool between batches.

Bake 12 minutes, or until glossy and cracked and edges are set. They will firm up as they cool, too.

Remove from oven and let sit on the pan for 2-3 minutes. Cool.

Oatmeal Cookies

¾ cup butter flavored shortening or dairy free butter, softened
1 cup brown sugar, packed
½ cup sugar
1 egg
¼ cup water
1 tsp. vanilla
1 cup gluten free all purpose flour*
½ tsp. xanthan gum (if not in flour)
1 tsp. salt
½ tsp. baking soda
3 cups gluten free oatmeal
½ cup dairy free chocolate chips, coconut, raisins or nuts (optional)

Preheat oven to 350°. Beat shortening, sugars, egg, water and vanilla together until creamy. Add flour, xanthan gum (if using), salt and baking soda. Add to creamed mixture. Blend well. Stir in oatmeal. Drop by teaspoonfuls onto greased cookie sheets. Bake 12-15 minutes. Makes 3 dozen.

Pumpkin Cookies

½ cup butter flavored shortening or dairy free butter
1 cup sugar
1 cup pumpkin
1 cup raisins
½ cup nuts
1 tsp. vanilla
1 tsp. baking soda
1 tsp. brown sugar
1 tsp. cinnamon
1 tsp. salt
2 cups gluten free all purpose flour
1 tsp. xanthan gum (if not in flour)

Preheat oven to 375°. Cream shortening, sugar and pumpkin in a bowl. Add the rest of the ingredients and mix well. Drop by small spoonfuls onto an ungreased cookie sheet. Brush tops with milk. Bake 8 minutes. Top with Buttercream Frosting (p.235). Makes 2 dozen.

Chocolate Chip Cookies

½   cup butter flavored shortening or dairy free butter
½   cup sugar
½   cup brown sugar, packed
1   egg
2   tsp. vanilla
½   tsp. baking soda
1   tsp. hot water
¼   tsp. salt
1½ cups gluten free all purpose flour
1   tsp. xanthan gum (if not in flour)
1   cups dairy free semi-sweet chocolate chips
½   cup chopped walnuts (optional)

Preheat oven to 350°. Cream together the shortening, sugar and brown sugar until smooth. Beat in the egg. Then stir in the vanilla.

Dissolve the baking soda in hot water. Add to the batter, along with the salt. Stir in flour, xanthan gum (if using), chocolate chips and nuts (if desired).

Drop by large spoonfuls onto ungreased pans. Bake12-15 minutes or until the edges are browned.

I am currently helping my son search for his chocolate that I ate last night.

Peanut Butter Cookies

1	cup shortening
1	cup sugar
1	cup brown sugar, packed
1	cup peanut butter
2	eggs
1	tsp. vanilla
3	cups gluten free all purpose flour
1	tsp. xanthan gum (if not in flour)
1	tsp. baking soda
½	tsp. salt

Preheat oven to 375°.

Cream shortening and sugars. Add peanut butter, eggs, vanilla and dry ingredients. Stir until well blended.

Roll into balls and place on a cookie sheet. Flatten with a fork dipped in flour. Turn fork 90° and make another fork print for the design.

Bake 10 minutes or until brown. Makes 6-8 dozen.

We are all brave in our own way.
For example I am not afraid to
eat raw cookie dough.

3 Ingredient Peanut Butter Cookies

1   cup minus 2 Tbsp. peanut butter
1   cup sugar
1   egg*

Preheat the oven to 350°. Stir the ingredients together until smooth. Scoop or roll 1 inch balls onto a cookie sheet. Press down with the back of a fork and then press again from the opposite direction to form the criss-cross pattern on top.

Bake 12 minutes and cool for 1-2 minutes before removing to a wire rack to finish cooling. Store in an airtight container.

*For cake cookies. An extra egg may be added to this recipe. If you choose to add an extra egg, simply scoop the finished cookie dough onto the baking tray. It will not be firm enough to roll into balls or press with a criss-cross pattern. The cookies will be puffier straight out of the oven and then will settle a bit as they cool.

Diet Day 1:

I have removed all bad food

from the house. It was delicious.

Soft Sugar Cookies

⅔ cup sugar
⅓ cup shortening
1 egg
⅓ tsp. vanilla
⅓ cup dairy free milk (rice or soy)
1 tsp. vinegar
1 tsp. baking powder
⅓ tsp. baking soda
2 cups gluten free all purpose flour
1 tsp. xanthan gum (if not in flour)

Preheat oven to 350°. Cream together the sugar, shortening, egg and vanilla. Add milk and vinegar. Mix well. Add dry ingredients. Mix until smooth.

Drop by tablespoons about 3 inches apart on a greased cookie sheet.

Wet fingers and press the cookies flat, about ¾ inch thickness. Place a drop or two of water on the top of each cookie and spread around. Then sprinkle sugar on top.

Bake 5-10 minutes. Let completely cool on cookie sheet before removing. Makes 4 dozen.

> Losing weight doesn't seem to be working for me so from now on I am going to concentrate and getting taller.

Fudge Brownies

¾   cup + 2 Tbsp. shortening
1½ cups granulated sugar
1   Tbsp. vanilla
3   eggs, room temperature
1   cup gluten free all purpose flour
½   tsp. xanthan gum (if not in flour)
¾   cup baking cocoa powder, (break lumps with fork)
¼   tsp. salt
¾   cup dairy free semi-sweet chocolate chips

Preheat the oven to 350°. Grease an 8×8 inch baking pan.

In a mixing bowl, stir together shortening, sugar and vanilla. Add eggs one at a time and stir until combined.

Add flour, xanthan gum (if using), cocoa powder and salt. Stir just until almost no streaks of flour remain. Do not overmix!

Fold in chocolate chips.

Pour the batter into the prepared pan. Bake 20-22 minutes or until the brownies have formed a thin crust and appear set in the middle. A toothpick inserted into the center will come out wet. A toothpick inserted into the sides will come out with some moist crumbs on it, but not totally raw batter.

The brownies will continue to bake as they sit in the pan and will firm up as they cool. Let cool completely. Then cover and store at room temperature for up to 4 days. You can also refrigerate them to give them a fudgier texture.

- **Use brownie crumbs for ice cream topping.**

Cake Brownies

⅓ cup cocoa, packed
½ cup plus 2 Tbsp. shortening
1 cup boiling water
2 cups gluten free all purpose flour
1 tsp. xanthan gum (if not in flour)
2 cups sugar
2 eggs, beaten
½ cup dairy free milk (rice or soy)
1 tsp. vinegar
1½ tsp. baking soda
½ tsp. salt

Preheat oven to 350°. Dissolve cocoa and shortening in boiling water. Mix all ingredients. Beat for 2 minutes. Pour into a well greased 9x13 inch pan floured with gluten free flour or two 9 inch pans. Bake 30-35 minutes or until a toothpick inserted into the center comes clean.

This tastes just like the package mix.

Apple Oatmeal Bars

1 cup oatmeal
½ tsp. salt
½ cup dairy free butter
1 cup gluten free all purpose flour
½ tsp. xanthan gum (if not in flour)
½ tsp. cinnamon
2½ cups apples, chopped or ¾ cup apple butter
     (omit cinnamon)
½ cup sugar

Preheat oven to 350°. Combine the first six ingredients and pat half into an 8x8 inch pan. Layer on apples and sugar. Crumble the remaining mixture on top. Bake 35 minutes. Makes 9 bars.

Lemon Bars

Crust

2   cups gluten free all purpose flour
1   tsp. xanthan gum (if not in flour)
1   cup butter flavored shortening or dairy free butter, melted
½   cup powdered sugar

Filling

4   eggs, well beaten
2   cups sugar
⅓   cup lemon juice
¼   cup gluten free all purpose flour
½   tsp. baking powder

Preheat oven to 350°. Mix all the crust ingredients in a bowl.

Press into greased 9x13 inch pan. Make sure the edges are higher than the center to contain the filling. Bake crust for 20 minutes or until it begins to brown.

Combine, eggs, sugar and lemon juice and mix well. Stir in flour and baking powder. Pour into baked crust and bake 20-30 minutes at 350°. The lemon bars are done when they are firm to the touch.

Cut into small squares and dust with powdered sugar. These bars are extremely rich so cut into small pieces. Makes 18 bars.

- **A pizza cutter makes cutting brownies a breeze. You can cut the pieces more evenly, and the brownies won't stick to the cutter.**

Baked Apples

1   apple, cored

Filling

1   Tbsp. honey or brown sugar
1   tsp. dairy free butter
     dash of cinnamon
     dash of nutmeg
     nuts and raisins (optional)

Preheat oven to 350°. Use 1 apple for each person. Fill the center of each apple with all filling ingredients. Bake until tender, or put in a Dutch oven on the stovetop and simmer on very low until tender. Serves 1.

Fried Apples

3   Tbsp. dairy free butter or bacon grease
4   large apples, cored and sliced
⅓   cup brown sugar
½   tsp. cinnamon

Cut apples into ¼ inch slices. Melt butter in a large skillet over medium-low heat. Put the apples, brown sugar and cinnamon in the skillet and cover.

Cook apple slices 7-10 minutes or until they begin to soften and the syrup thickens. Serve coated with excess syrup on top. Serves 4.

Apple Crisp

6 apples, peeled and sliced
1 cup brown sugar
½ cup gluten free oatmeal
½ cup gluten free all purpose flour
½ cup dairy free butter, softened
1 tsp. cinnamon and/or nutmeg
¼ cup water

Preheat oven to 350°. Arrange apples in a well greased baking dish. Blend all remaining ingredients except water. Spread evenly over the top of the apples. Pour water over the topping.

Bake 45 minutes until apples are tender and the top is crisp.
Serves 6.

Peach Crisp

Use peaches in place of apples.

- **Try adding ¼ to ½ teaspoon baking soda and half the amount of sugar when making sweet desserts.** The baking soda brings out the sweetness of the sugar so you can use less.

- **Pour boiling water over pecans in the shell** and let them sit 30 minutes. When you shell them, they should come out whole.

- **Dried out coconut can be revitalized by sprinkling with milk.** Let it stand until it regains its freshness.

- **To soften brown sugar, place a slice of bread or an apple slice in the bag and seal.**

Fruits Dipped In Chocolate

1   bag of dairy free white, dark, semi-sweet or milk chocolate chips

Fruit suggestions:

strawberries
kiwi
banana
grapes
melon (use a small scoop, towel dry)
pineapple
mango
orange and grapefruit slices, whole and skinned
papaya

Melt the chocolate chips in a bowl in the microwave or in a double boiler. Put the dry fruit on the end of a toothpick or skewer. Dip the fruit in the chocolate and then briefly let the excess chocolate drip off. Place the fruits on a sheet of waxed paper to harden.

I burn about 2000 calories

every time I put

fitted sheets on by myself.

Red Jello Salad

This recipe is a family favorite and a staple for Christmas! Our family says we can't celebrate Christmas without the Red Jello Salad! ;-)
It adds a beautiful red color to the Christmas table and children and men seem to really love it.

½   cup boiling water
1   small pkg. cherry Jello
¼-½ cup red hot candies
1½ cups applesauce

Dissolve Jello and candies in boiling water. I usually do this in a small saucepan so I can keep it on low heat and it warm while dissolving the candies. When mostly dissolved, add the applesauce and chill until set.

- **Desserts are not needed every night.** Serve them only one or two times a week or only on weekends. This not only saves money, but it also saves calories.

- **Dried out raisins or other fruit may be plumped** by soaking in juice or water.

- **To dress up desserts:** Place chocolate syrup, lemon curd or other sauces into squirt bottles. This makes it easier to decorate cakes, fruit dishes or other desserts.

Funnel Cakes

1½	cups gluten free all purpose flour
½	tsp. xanthan gum (if not in flour)
2	Tbsp. sugar
1½	tsp. baking powder
	pinch salt
¼	tsp. cinnamon
1	egg
½-¾	cup dairy free milk* (rice or soy)
½	cup water
¼	tsp. vanilla
	vegetable oil
	powdered sugar, glaze or nuts as desired

Mix dry ingredients. Add egg, milk, water and vanilla. Stir until smooth.

Pour oil into a skillet and heat to 375°.

Holding your finger over the end of a funnel, pour in ¼ cup batter. Holding over the hot oil, remove your finger and let the batter drizzle over the hot oil. As the batter flows, move the funnel in a circle to form a spiral cake.

Fry about 2 minutes on each side, turning once, until golden brown. Remove from oil and drain. Sprinkle with powdered sugar, glaze or nuts. Makes 6 cakes.

*If batter is too thick for your funnel, add additional ¼-½ cup milk.

> "If at first you don't succeed,
>
> destroy all evidence that you ever tried."

Granola Bars

¾ cup brown sugar
½ cup sugar
½ cup dairy free butter, softened
2 Tbsp. honey or corn syrup
½ tsp. vanilla
1 egg
1 cup gluten free all purpose flour
½ tsp. xanthan gum (if not in flour)
1 tsp. cinnamon
½ tsp. baking soda
¼ tsp. salt
1½ cups gluten free oatmeal
1¼ cups gluten free crispy rice cereal, corn flakes
      or crushed graham crackers
1 cup dairy free chocolate chips*

Preheat oven to 350°. In a large bowl, cream sugars and butter until fluffy. Add honey, vanilla and egg. Mix well. Blend in flour, xanthan gum (if using), cinnamon, baking soda and salt. Stir in remaining ingredients. Press firmly into the bottom of a greased 9x13 inch pan. Bake 20-25 minutes.

To microwave: Press ingredients into a microwave safe dish. Microwave on medium power for 7-9 minutes. Rotate dish every three minutes. The bars will firm as they stand. Cool and cut into bars. Save the crumbs for yogurt or ice cream topping. Makes 24 bars.

* The following may be used in addition to or to replace chocolate chips:

1 cup coconut
½ cup creamy or chunky peanut butter
½ cup nuts
½-1 cup raisins, dried apples or apricots
½ cup fruit preserves

Popcorn Balls

40   large marshmallows
¼   cup dairy free butter
     food coloring (optional)
8-10 cups popped popcorn, old maids and hulls removed

Melt marshmallows and butter over low heat. Add food coloring and mix well.

Pour popped corn into a large bowl. Place marshmallow mixture over popcorn while stirring. Mix well to coat all of the popped corn. Butter your hands to form the popcorn mixture into balls. Makes 8-10 popcorn balls.

Peanut Caramel Popcorn
(just like Cracker Jacks)

1   cup dairy free butter
2   cups brown sugar
½   cup light or dark corn syrup
1   tsp. salt
1   tsp. baking soda
1   tsp. vanilla
6   qts. popped corn
½-1 cup peanuts

Melt dairy free butter in a large saucepan. Stir in brown sugar, corn syrup and salt.

Bring to a boil, stirring constantly. Then boil without stirring for 5 minutes.

Remove from heat. Stir in baking soda and vanilla. Gradually pour over popped corn and peanuts. Mix until coated. Makes 6 quarts.

Pineapple Orange Gelatin

1   pkg. unflavored gelatin
1   cup cold water
3   Tbsp. sugar
2   Tbsp. frozen orange juice concentrate
    drained juice from pineapple chunks plus
        water to make 1¼ cups
1   cup pineapple chunks, drained
1   banana, sliced (optional)

Combine gelatin, cold water and sugar in a saucepan. Heat to dissolve gelatin.

Add the orange juice concentrate, pineapple juice and water. Stir until blended. Fold in fruit. Chill until set. Serves 6.

Rice Pudding

½   cup rice, uncooked
4   cups dairy free milk (rice, almond or coconut)
½   tsp. cinnamon
½   tsp. nutmeg
¼   cup sugar
½   tsp. salt
½   cup raisins (optional)

Combine all the ingredients except raisins and pour into a greased baking dish. Bake at 275° for 3 hours. Stir frequently during the first hour. The mixture should not boil. Add raisins during the last ½ hour. Serve either hot or cold. Serves 6.

Apple Snack

2   qts. apples, peeled, cored and halved

Coarsely grate apples. Place on a greased cookie sheet. Bake at 225° until dry. Remove from cookie sheet and break into pieces. Store in an airtight container.

Frozen Bananas

bananas
skewers (optional)

Cut bananas in half crosswise. Insert skewer in the thicker end. Place bananas on a tray and place in freezer. When frozen, move to a plastic bag and keep frozen until ready to use.

Toppings

dairy free yogurt   peanut butter

melted dairy free chocolate   applesauce

nuts, finely chopped   coconut

Allow bananas to thaw slightly. Put toppings in small bowls. Dip banana before each bite. Eat plain or roll or dip into any of the toppings. Use the wet topping first so the others will stick.

Frozen Grapes

Wash and separate the grapes. Drain and put on cookie sheet. Freeze. Store in freezer bags. Give to kids as frozen treats.
Note: Do not thaw. The grapes become mushy when thawed.

Yogurt Popsicles

2   cups plain dairy free yogurt
1   (6 oz.) can frozen orange juice concentrate
1   tsp. vanilla
6   oz. water

Blend ingredients together in a blender and then freeze in popsicle molds. Makes 8-10 popsicles.

Popsicle Ideas

- fruit: bananas, applesauce, blackberries, blueberries, strawberries, raspberries

- dairy free yogurt

- gelatin

- syrup from canned fruit

- food coloring for added pizzazz

- **For popsicle molds, use small waxed paper cups. Insert sticks into paper cup molds when partially frozen. To serve, peel off the paper cup.**

Pudding Pops

1   pkg. cook and serve pudding
3   cups dairy free milk (rice or soy)

Combine 1 large package of pudding with 3 cups of milk. Mix only enough to blend well. Quickly pour into popsicle molds and freeze. Chocolate and vanilla pudding may be layered for a fun treat. Makes 8-10 popsicles.

*You can use regular homemade pudding instead of store bought pudding mix if you prefer.

Fudgesicles

½   cup sugar
2   Tbsp. cornstarch
3   Tbsp. cocoa
⅛   tsp. salt
2   eggs, slightly beaten
2½   cups dairy free milk (rice or soy)
2   Tbsp. dairy free butter
2   tsp. vanilla

Mix sugar, cornstarch, cocoa and salt in a 2 quart saucepan. Add eggs to the sugar mixture and slowly stir in milk until combined.

Cook over medium heat, stirring constantly, until the mixture thickens and boils. Boil and stir 1 minute.

Remove from heat. Stir in butter and vanilla. Quickly pour into popsicle molds and freeze. Makes 8-10 Fudgesicles.

Snow Cones

      snow, fresh and clean
1   pkg. flavored drink mix (flavor of your choice)

Mix drink mix according to directions, using only half the water called for. Chill 1 hour.

Just before serving, go out and get some fresh, clean snow. Pack snow into cups. Pour chilled drink mix over the snow and serve.

You can also use fruit juice boiled down to half with food coloring added. Chill juice before adding to snow.

Apple juice: green or red food coloring

Grape juice: purple food coloring

Snow Ice Cream

½   cup dairy free milk (rice or soy)
¼   cup sugar
¼   tsp. vanilla
2   cereal bowls fresh clean snow

Mix milk, sugar and vanilla together. Stir until vanilla is dissolved. Add fresh snow and stir gently until it is thoroughly mixed. Serve immediately. Serves 4.

Strawberry Leather

3   cups fresh or frozen strawberries*
1   Tbsp. lemon juice
1   Tbsp. light corn syrup

Place strawberries in a blender and process until smooth. Measure 2 cups of strawberry puree. Stir in lemon juice and corn syrup.

Line a 15x10x1 inch jellyroll pan with heavy duty plastic wrap and tape plastic wrap to the pan at the corners. Pour strawberry mixture in prepared pan and spread thin, leaving 1 inch on all sides.

You can adjust this to fit your dehydrator or another pan. Be sure it is spread thin on the pan. Dry in an oven or dehydrator at 150° for 7-8 hours or until surface is no longer sticky.

Remove leather from pan while still warm and roll up jellyroll fashion. Cut into logs and wrap in plastic wrap. Makes five 2 inch logs.

*Any other fruit may be used in place of the strawberries.

There are 3 kinds of people in this world.

Those who are good at math

and those who aren't.

Vanilla Pudding

⅓   cup sugar
2   Tbsp. cornstarch
⅛   tsp. salt
2   eggs, slightly beaten
2   cups dairy free milk (almond or coconut)
2   Tbsp. dairy free butter
2   tsp. vanilla

Mix sugar, cornstarch and salt in a 2 quart saucepan. Add eggs to sugar mixture and slowly stir in milk until combined.

Cook over medium heat, stirring constantly, until mixture thickens and boils. Boil and stir 1 minute. Remove from heat. Stir in butter and vanilla. Cool slightly.

Pour into dessert dishes and chill. You can also top with nuts or whipped topping. Serves 4-6.

Chocolate Pudding

Stir 3 tablespoons cocoa into sugar cornstarch mixture.

Chocolate Peanut Butter Pudding

Stir ¼ cup peanut butter into chocolate pudding. Omit butter.

Butterscotch Pudding

Substitute ⅔ cup packed brown sugar for the sugar and decrease vanilla to 1 teaspoon.

Butterscotch Sauce

½   cup dairy free butter
2   cups brown sugar, packed
1   cup dairy free milk (canned coconut works best)

Melt butter in a saucepan. Add brown sugar and milk. Cook on medium heat, stirring constantly, until blended. Keep refrigerated. Great on top of ice cream. Makes 2 cups.

Peanut Butterscotch Sauce

Add ½ cup peanut butter with brown sugar and milk.

Hot Fudge Sauce

½   cup packed plus 1 Tbsp. cocoa
¼   tsp salt
¾   cup dairy free butter
1½   cups dairy free milk (rice or soy)
2   cups sugar
1-2 Tbsp. cornstarch*
1   tsp. vanilla

Mix all ingredients except vanilla in a saucepan and heat to a rolling boil. Boil 1 minute. Remove from heat and add vanilla. Serve warm or chilled. The sauce will thicken as it cools. Makes 3 cups.

*Dairy free milks don't get as thick as cow's milk. Cornstarch helps to thicken it up. Use less cornstarch for a thinner hot fudge and more for a thicker hot fudge.

Caramel Sauce

2   egg yolks, beaten
¼   cup dairy free butter
½   cup brown sugar, packed
½   cup water
¼   cup sugar
1   tsp. vanilla

In a saucepan, heat all ingredients to boiling, stirring constantly. Boil 1 minute. Serve warm or cold. Makes 1 cup.

Chocolate Syrup

½   cup cocoa, packed
1   cup water
2   cups sugar
⅛   tsp. salt
¼   tsp. vanilla

Mix cocoa and water in a saucepan. Heat and stir to dissolve the cocoa. Add the sugar and stir to dissolve. Boil 3 minutes. Add the salt and vanilla. Pour into a sterilized jar. Store covered in the refrigerator. Keeps for several months. Makes 2 cups.

Coconut Whipped Cream

1   can full-fat coconut milk
1-3 Tbsp. powdered sugar (or to taste)
½   tsp. vanilla

Refrigerate coconut milk overnight in the can. When ready to use, open can carefully so you don't mix the coconut milk with the coconut fat. Gently remove the hardened coconut fat off the top* of the can and place in a bowl. (Save the milk.)

Whip coconut fat until thick and creamy, up to 3-4 minutes. If chunky, add a bit of the leftover coconut milk to smooth it out. Add powdered sugar and vanilla, to taste. Whip until well blended. Serve.

You can store this coconut whipped cream in the refrigerator up to 2 weeks.

*If you don't have hardened fat on the top of your coconut milk, you probably got one with added water or "light" coconut milk. To tell if it's full fat, it should have 130 calories for ⅓ cup on the nutrition label.

Occasionally, the coconut cream will just not set up. Chill 2 cans of full fat coconut cream in case one doesn't work out.

Miscellaneous

Miscellaneous Tips

- **If honey becomes crystallized or cloudy,** it is still good. Just warm it up in the microwave or in a pan of boiling water for a few minutes. Stir until it becomes clear again.

- **If jelly or jam doesn't set up well,** use for popsicles or add more water, boil and make syrup.

- **Put seasoned salt, taco seasonings, etc. in old spice bottles** to make them more convenient to use. Make sure to re-label bottles.

- **To make chopped garlic:** Peel and dice garlic and put in a small glass jar. Press down on the garlic with the back of a spoon and place 2 tablespoons olive oil on top. Seal and refrigerate. Keep for one to two weeks.

- **Store garlic in a jar or bottle of vegetable oil.** This will keep the garlic from drying out and then you will have garlic flavored oil for salads. Use within one week.

- **To make an all-in-one salt and pepper shaker:** Place 1 part pepper to 6 parts salt in an old spice jar or salt shaker.

- **Raw potatoes will take food stains off of your fingers. Just slice the potato and rub on the stains. Then rinse your fingers with water.**

Almond Milk

1   cup raw almonds
5   cups filtered water (less to thicken, more to thin)
1   pinch salt

Soak almonds in water overnight or 2 hours in very hot water. Add soaked almonds, water, salt and any additional add-ins (optional) to a high-speed blender. Blend 1-2 minutes, until creamy and smooth.

Lay a clean dish towel over a mixing bowl. Pour almond milk mixture to strain through the towel. Carefully gather the corners, lift up and squeeze until all of the liquid is extracted. Discard pulp and save for adding to baked goods (especially crackers).

Transfer to a covered bottle or jar and refrigerate. Will keep for up to 4-5 days. Shake well before drinking as it tends to separate.

Variations

- **Sweetened Almond Milk** - Add 2 Tbsp. sugar or 2 whole dates or 2 Tbsp. honey or agave.

- **Vanilla Almond Milk** - Add 1 tsp. vanilla extract.

- **Chocolate Almond Milk** - Add 2 Tbsp. baking cocoa powder plus 2 Tbsp. sugar.

- **Berry Almond Milk** - Add ½ cup berries.

Coconut Milk

2   cups shredded unsweetened coconut
3-4 cups water (use less water for thicker, creamier milk)
      pinch salt

Add coconut, 3 cups water, salt and any additional add-ins to a blender. Top with lid and blend 2 minutes or until well combined.

Test sweetness. Add more sugar, salt, or vanilla as desired. Add remaining 1 cup water if too thick.

Pour the mixture over a large mixing bowl or pitcher covered with a thin towel. Pull sides of towel up and gently squeeze liquid out. Save pulp for baked goods or to add to oatmeal, smoothies or energy bites.

Store in a sealed container and refrigerate. Will keep in the refrigerator up to 5 days. Shake before use.

Variations

- **Sweetened Coconut Milk** - 1 Tbsp. sugar or 1 date or 1 Tbsp. maple syrup or 1 Tbsp. agave

- **Vanilla Coconut Milk** - ½ tsp. vanilla

- **Chocolate Coconut Milk** - 2 Tbsp. cocoa

- **Berry Coconut Milk** - ¼ cup fresh berries

Oat Milk

3   cups water
1   Tbsp. sugar (optional)
½   cup gluten free rolled oats
     pinch of salt

Add the water and oats in blender and until the oats have broken down and the liquid looks creamy, about 20 to 30 seconds.

DO NOT OVERBLEND.

Pour the blended mixture through a fine mesh strainer, and tap the sides of the strainer to make sure the liquid strains through. (Don't use a spoon to press the pulp into the sides of the strainer, or the resulting milk will be slimy.

Use the milk right away, or store it in an airtight container in the fridge for up to 4 days.

Cashew Milk

1   cup raw cashews
4   cups water, divided*
1-2 Tbsp. sugar or sweetener of your choice
2   tsp. vanilla
     dash salt
     pinch of cinnamon (optional)

Soak the cashews in water at least 4 hours, or overnight in the refrigerator. Drain and rinse until the water runs clear. Add the cashews and two cups water to a blender. Start on a low setting and increase the speed until the cashews are totally pulverized, about 2 minutes (or longer, if needed).

Blend 2 cups more water (less for a thicker milk), sweetener, vanilla, salt and cinnamon (optional). When blended, strain through a fine mesh strainer or cheese cloth. Store the milk in a covered container in the refrigerator. It should keep for 3 to 4 days.

Rice Milk

1   cup rice, cooked
4   cups water

Blend rice and water in a blender until smooth, approximately 1 minute. Blend again for ultra-smooth consistency. Store in the refrigerator and enjoy cold. Shake before using.

Baking Powder

2   tsp. cream of tartar
1   tsp. baking soda

Mix together and use immediately. Mix into batter quickly and put in oven right away.

*If you want to mix ahead of time, add 1 teaspoon cornstarch and store no longer than one month.

*If you have a recipe that calls for double-acting baking powder, use twice the amount.

Homemade baking powder starts to fizz and release carbon dioxide the minute it is added to liquid.

Egg Substitute

1   heaping Tbsp. soy flour or powder OR ground flax seed
1   Tbsp. water

This is a great substitute for eggs in baking. Equals 1 egg.

Powdered Sugar

1   cup granulated sugar
1   tsp. cornstarch

Combine granulated sugar and cornstarch in a blender or food processor. Blend 1 minute or until powdered.

Self Rising Flour

4   cups gluten free all purpose flour
2   tsp. salt
2   Tbsp. double-acting baking powder

Mix well and store in an airtight container. Use in recipes calling for self rising flour. Makes 4 cups.

Vanilla

2   vanilla beans cut lengthwise (but not in half)
¾   cup vodka

Combine the ingredients in a ½ pint jar and set aside to steep for 3 or 4 weeks. Use vanilla as usual. When the level of the vanilla drops below the vanilla beans, add more vodka. You can get 4-5 large bottles worth of vanilla out of 2 beans.

Pumpkin Pie Spice

½   tsp. cinnamon
¼   tsp. nutmeg
⅛   tsp. ginger
⅛   tsp. cloves

Mix well. Makes 1 teaspoon. Use in any recipe calling for pumpkin pie spice.

Bouquet Garni Bags

bay leaf
sprig of thyme
parsley leaves

Place a few sprigs of each in a cheesecloth and tie. Use in stocks, soups, and stews.

Cajun Seasoning

1   Tbsp. paprika
2½   tsp. salt
1   tsp. onion powder
1   tsp. garlic powder
1   tsp. cayenne pepper
¾   tsp. white pepper
¾   tsp. black pepper
½   tsp. thyme leaves, dried
½   tsp. oregano, dried

Combine ingredients and mix well. Store in an airtight container.

Seasoned Salt

8   Tbsp. salt
3   Tbsp. pepper
2   Tbsp. paprika
½   Tbsp. onion powder
½   Tbsp. garlic powder

Mix all ingredients in a bowl. Store in an airtight container.

Taco Seasoning

6   tsp. chili powder
4½   tsp. cumin
5   tsp. paprika
¼   tsp. oregano
3   tsp. onion powder
2½   tsp. garlic powder
⅛-¼   tsp. cayenne pepper

Mix all ingredients and store in an airtight container. One teaspoon of homemade taco seasoning equals 2 teaspoons store bought.

Italian Seasoning

¼   cup dried basil
2   Tbsp. dried marjoram
2   Tbsp. dried oregano
2   Tbsp. dried coriander
2   Tbsp. dried thyme
2   Tbsp. dried rosemary
2   tsp. garlic powder
1   tsp. sugar

Combine all the ingredients. Store in an airtight container in a cool dark place for up to 3 months.

Gluten Free
Shake And Bake

4   cups gluten free all purpose flour
4   cups gluten free crackers, crushed
4   Tbsp. salt
2   Tbsp. sugar
2   tsp. garlic powder
2   tsp. onion powder
3   Tbsp. paprika
¼   cup vegetable oil

Mix well and store indefinitely in the refrigerator in a covered container.

To use: Moisten the chicken pieces with dairy free milk (rice or soy) or water. Pour about 2 cups mixture (or more, if needed) into a plastic bag. Place chicken pieces, one at a time, into the bag and shake until evenly coated.

Preheat oven to 350° and bake coated chicken pieces in a greased shallow pan for 45-60 minutes. Discard plastic bag with unused coating. DO NOT reuse extra coating that has come into contact with raw chicken!

I hate it when people see me at the grocery store
and say "Hey what are you doing here."
So I just say, "Hunting for elephants."

Chili Sauce

1   gal. can tomatoes, diced
1-2   medium onions, diced
1   tsp. cinnamon
1   tsp. dry mustard
1   cup sugar
½   tsp. curry powder
½-1   cup vinegar
½   tsp. nutmeg
      chili powder (to taste)
5   tsp. salt

Cook tomatoes and onions until soft. Strain through a colander. Add back to the pot, along with the rest of the ingredients and cook down to desired consistency. Can or freeze in 2 cup portions. Makes 10 pints.

Cranberry Sauce

1   (15 oz.) can jellied cranberry sauce
1   tsp. mustard
2   Tbsp. lemon juice
¼   tsp. ground cloves

Mix together. Makes a great topping for ham or turkey. Makes 1¼ cups.

Easy Barbecue Sauce

1   cup grape jelly
     garlic or garlic powder (to taste)
1   cup ketchup

Mix together and serve with ribs or chicken wings. Makes 2 cups.

Grandma's Barbecue Sauce

2   cups ketchup
1½   cups brown sugar
1   Tbsp. onion, finely chopped or ½ tsp. onion salt
½   tsp. garlic powder
2   Tbsp. liquid smoke

Mix all the ingredients in a bowl. Place in a jar and store in the refrigerator. Makes 3 cups.

Hickory Barbecue Sauce

1   (20 oz.) bottle ketchup
1   tsp. salt
½   cup water
1   tsp. onion powder
¼   cup cider vinegar
1-4   tsp. liquid smoke (to taste)
1   Tbsp. brown sugar, packed
⅛   tsp. garlic powder
1   Tbsp. Worcestershire sauce

Blend all the ingredients in a blender until smooth. Store in the refrigerator. Use on anything when you want a barbecue flavor. Makes 3½ cups.

Ketchup

1   (8 oz.) can tomato sauce
3   Tbsp. sugar
    very small dash of cinnamon
1   Tbsp. plus 1 tsp. vinegar

Pour tomato sauce into a small saucepan and boil away some of the water until it begins to thicken. Add the sugar, cinnamon and vinegar. Simmer for 3 to 4 minutes longer. Refrigerate.

Warning: Go easy on the cinnamon because it's easy to put in too much. Makes 1 cup.

Ham Sauce

1   cup dairy free sour cream
2   Tbsp. prepared mustard
1   Tbsp. horseradish

Add horseradish and mustard to sour cream. Stir well. Serve with slow cooked ham. Makes 1 cup.

My Saturday was going really well until I realized it was Sunday.

Mayonnaise

1   egg, cold
¾   cup + 2½ Tbsp. canola or sunflower oil, cold
2   Tbsp. white vinegar or lemon juice
¼   tsp. salt
1   tsp. Dijon mustard (optional)

Put all of the ingredients into a tall, narrow container in this order: egg (be careful not to break the yolk), oil, white vinegar, salt and Dijon mustard. (I used the container that came with my immersion blender.)

Insert the immersion blender and push it all the way to the bottom of the jar. Turn it on at the highest speed and DO NOT move the blender for 10 seconds.

Almost instantly, the mixture will begin to emulsify and look like mayonnaise. Now you can move the immersion blender up and down to incorporate any oil that is sitting on the top. Keep it refrigerated and use within one week.

Garlic Mayo

1   cup mayonnaise
2   large cloves garlic, pressed, or ½ tsp. garlic powder

Mix pressed garlic with mayonnaise. Refrigerate for at least one day before using. Great on sandwiches, chicken, fish or with vegetables. Makes 1 cup. Use within 1 week.

Homemade Horseradish

fresh horseradish, peeled and chopped
water
vinegar

Place horseradish in a food processor. Process to the texture you desire, adding water and white vinegar as necessary to get the taste you want. Store in covered jars in the refrigerator for several months.

Horseradish Mayo

1   cup mayonnaise
1   tsp. to 1 Tbsp. horseradish (to taste)

Mix ingredients together. Use on sandwiches, ham or roast beef. Keeps several weeks in the refrigerator.

An antique store sign:
Come in and buy
what your grandmother threw away.

Dijon Mustard

2   cups dry wine
1   large onion, chopped
3   cloves garlic, pressed
1   cup dry mustard
3   Tbsp. honey
1   Tbsp. vegetable oil
2   tsp. salt

Combine wine, onion and garlic in a saucepan. Bring to a boil and simmer 5 minutes.

Cool, strain and discard solids. Add mustard to the liquid and stir until smooth. Blend in honey, oil and salt. Return to saucepan and heat slowly until thickened, stirring constantly.

Cool in the refrigerator in a covered jar. Age 6 to 8 weeks in a cool, dark place. Refrigerate after aging. Makes 2 cups.

Mustard

½   cup mustard seeds
     dash of salt
     dash of turmeric
¼   cup cider vinegar
½   cup water

Grind mustard seeds, salt and turmeric in a food processor. Combine the mustard mixture with cider vinegar and water in the top of a double boiler. Cook and stir until smooth. Cool and thin as needed with water and/or cider vinegar. Makes ¾ cup.

Mustard Sauce

1   Tbsp. dairy free butter
1   Tbsp. cornstarch
¼   tsp. pepper
1   cup dairy free milk (rice or soy)
3   Tbsp. prepared mustard
1   Tbsp. prepared horseradish

Heat butter over low heat in a 1½ quart saucepan until melted. Stir in cornstarch and pepper, stirring constantly, until smooth and bubbly.

Remove from heat. Stir in milk. Heat to boiling, stirring constantly. Boil and stir 1 minute. Stir in mustard and horseradish.

Serve warm. Great with smoked sausage, steak bites, or cooked cabbage. Makes 1 cup.

Horseradish Mustard

1   cup dry mustard
1   Tbsp. lemon juice
¼   cup honey
¼   tsp. lemon peel, grated
½   tsp. salt
5   Tbsp. horseradish
½   cup vinegar
¼   cup oil

Combine all the ingredients in a food processor and mix well. Put the horseradish mustard in jars and seal. Age 2-8 weeks in the refrigerator. Makes 1¼ cups.

Hot Mustard

1   cup dry mustard
2   Tbsp. honey
¼   tsp. corn oil
½   cup water

Mix ingredients. Seal in a jar. Age 2 weeks in a cool, dark place and then refrigerate. Makes 1¼ cups.

Hot Mustard Sauce

¼   cup ground mustard
¼   cup vinegar
¼   cup sugar
1   egg yolk
2   Tbsp. honey
    gluten free pretzels

In a small saucepan, combine mustard and vinegar. Let stand for 30 minutes. Whisk in the sugar and the egg yolk, until smooth. Cook over medium heat, whisking constantly, just until mixture begins to simmer and is thickened (about 7 minutes).

Remove from heat and whisk in the honey. Chill. Serve with pretzels.

Store in the refrigerator. Makes ½ cup.

Salsa

4   large ripe tomatoes
3   cans tomato paste
4   large green tomatoes, skinned
1½   cups vinegar
1   large green pepper, chopped
2   Tbsp. brown sugar
2   onions, chopped
12   jalapeno peppers, seeded and chopped (leave seeds in for hot flavor)
4   tsp. garlic powder or 6-8 garlic cloves, chopped

Thoroughly process all ingredients in a food processor. Place in a large Dutch oven and bring to a boil. Can. If your family eats a lot of salsa, there is no need to can it. Just refrigerate. Makes 6 pints.

Steak Dip

1   cup dairy free sour cream
1   tsp. lemon juice
2-4 Tbsp. horseradish (to taste)
½-1 tsp. garlic powder (to taste)
1   tsp. Worcestershire sauce

Mix ingredients together. Great for dipping pieces of slow cooked round steak. Makes 1 cup.

Shrimp Cocktail

1   cup ketchup
¼   tsp. Worcestershire sauce (¼ tsp. more to taste)
1   tsp. lemon juice
1½   tsp. horseradish (more to taste)
1   Tbsp. honey

Mix ingredients together. Stir well. Refrigerate any leftovers. Makes 1 cup.

Sweet And Sour Sauce

¼   cup brown sugar, packed
1   Tbsp. cornstarch
2   Tbsp. white vinegar
2   Tbsp. gluten free soy sauce
¾   cup ketchup
⅓   cup reserved pineapple juice
1   can pineapple chunks (optional)

Mix the brown sugar and cornstarch in a saucepan. Add the rest of the ingredients except the pineapple. Heat and stir until it boils and thickens. Add pineapple and serve. Great with pork or chicken. Makes 1¼ cups.

Tartar Sauce

1   cup salad dressing (Miracle Whip)
¼   cup sweet relish

Combine ingredients. Mix well and refrigerate. Makes 1 cup.

It's often not a slow metabolism

that makes us put on weight,

but a fast fork.

Popcorn

2   Tbsp. vegetable oil
1½ cups popcorn

Heat oil in a large covered pan. Place 3 kernels popcorn in the pan. When the kernels pop, pour in the popcorn. Reduce heat to medium. Cover and shake until popping slows to 1 pop every 3-4 seconds. Remove from the pan and season as desired. Makes 9-10 cups.

Popcorn Seasonings

Pour ¼ cup melted dairy free butter over popcorn and sprinkle with any of the following:

- salt
- dairy free Parmesan cheese
- garlic powder
- onion powder
- chili powder
- dairy free Cheddar cheese, finely grated

Barbecue Flavored Popcorn

2   tsp. dried parsley
2   tsp. paprika
½   tsp. hickory smoke salt
½   tsp. onion powder
¼   tsp. garlic powder

Mix and pour over popcorn.

Spiced Popcorn

1   tsp. paprika
½   tsp. crushed red pepper
½   tsp. cumin
⅓   cup dairy free Parmesan cheese
¼   cup dairy free butter, melted

Mix together and pour over popcorn.

Kettle Corn

2   Tbsp. vegetable oil
½   cup popcorn
3   Tbsp. white sugar

Heat oil on medium in pan until hot. Add popcorn and sprinkle all of the sugar over it. Cover and shake continuously until popped.

•   **Popcorn should be stored in the freezer. It lasts longer and pops more kernels.**

Roasted Sunflower Seeds

2   cups hulled sunflower seeds
1   Tbsp. oil
1   tsp. Worcestershire sauce
¼   tsp. salt
     garlic salt (to taste)
     onion salt (to taste)

Preheat oven to 325°. Mix until blended well. Place a thin layer on a cookie sheet. Bake 30 minutes, stirring occasionally. Seeds are done when they are lightly browned and crunchy. Makes 2 cups.

Roasted Pumpkin Seeds

Preheat oven to 250°. Boil seeds in water for 5 minutes. Drain well. Sprinkle with salt or seasoned salt. Place a thin layer on a cookie sheet. Bake 30 minutes. Stir. Bake ½-1 hour more or until crunchy.

*Squash seeds may also be used.

Baked Tortilla Chips

    corn tortillas
    spray oil
    salt
    garlic powder (optional)
    onion powder (optional)
    chili powder (optional)

Preheat oven to 275°. Spray tortillas very lightly with oil. Sprinkle with seasonings, if desired. Place on oven rack and bake 20-30 minutes or until crispy.

Sprinkle with salt and break apart into pieces when cooled.

If you want more uniform pieces, cut tortillas* in quarters after spraying on the oil. Then bake on a cookie sheet. If you like, flavor with garlic powder, onion powder or chili powder.

*A pizza cutter makes it easy to cut several tortillas at a time.

Fried Tortilla Chips

    corn tortillas
    oil for frying
    salt (optional)

Cut tortillas* into wedges. Heat 1 inch of oil in a frying pan. Fry several wedges until crisp on both sides. Remove with a slotted spoon and drain on paper towels. Sprinkle with salt if desired.

*A pizza cutter makes it easy to cut several tortillas at a time.

Graham Crackers

1½   cups brown rice flour
½   cup cornstarch
⅓   cup dark brown sugar
1   tsp. baking powder
½   tsp. salt
5   Tbsp. butter flavored shortening, cold
6   Tbsp. dairy free milk (rice or soy)
3   Tbsp. honey

Preheat oven to 350°. Whisk dry ingredients together in a medium mixing bowl. Cut cold shortening into flour mixture by rubbing the shortening between your fingers. Add milk and honey. Stir.

Turn dough out onto a lightly rice floured piece of 12x16 inch parchment paper. Pat dough into a rectangle. Dust the top of the dough lightly with rice flour. Place another 12x16 inch piece of parchment paper on top of the dough. Roll dough out until it covers all of the paper. Dough rectangle will be about ⅛ inch thick.

Carefully remove top piece of parchment paper. Transfer dough, with bottom parchment paper, to a 12 x 18 baking pan.

Using a pizza cutter, score the dough into rectangles. Rectangles should be 6x2¾ inches in size for "standard" graham crackers and 3x2¾ inches for a "s'more" size graham cracker. The graham crackers will break apart after baking. Do not worry if the dough seems to still be touching after scoring with the pizza cutter. Prick dough all over with a fork.

Chill dough for 10 minutes. Bake for 15 minutes or until evenly brown.

Remove graham crackers from the pan and place on a wire rack to cool. Allow crackers to cool completely. Break along scored lines.

Homemade Crackers

1   cup gluten free all purpose flour
½   tsp. sugar
½   tsp. salt
1   Tbsp. dairy free butter
½-¼ cup water

Preheat oven to 400°. Mix together flour, sugar and salt. Cut in butter with 2 knives or your fingertips until the mixture looks like coarse crumbs. Stir in enough water to make a stiff dough. If too dry, add more water.

Place lightly floured dough between two pieces of parchment paper on a cookie sheet. Roll about ¼ inch thick. Remove top piece of parchment paper and cut into squares with a pizza cutter. Prick with a fork several times on each cracker. Sprinkle water on top, smoothing out tops and sprinkle with coarse salt if desired. Bake 15-20 minutes.

Honey Butter

½   cup dairy free butter, softened
½   cup honey

Mix together until smooth. Store, covered, in the refrigerator. Great with cornbread, crackers or bread. Makes 1 cup.

Garlic Butter

½   cup dairy free butter, softened
½   tsp. garlic powder or 2 cloves garlic, finely chopped

Mix together until smooth. Store in a covered container in the refrigerator. Makes ½ cup.

Spiced Honey

1   lemon
12   whole cloves
3   sticks cinnamon
3   cups honey

Cut lemon into 6 thin slices. Place all ingredients in a saucepan and bring to a boil, stirring occasionally.

Remove lemon slices and discard cloves. Place 2 lemon slices and 1 cinnamon stick in each jar. Ladle hot honey into jars, leaving ¼ inch head space.

Screw on lids and process for 10 minutes in boiling water canner. Makes 3 half pints.

Better to remain silent
and be thought a fool
than to open your mouth
and remove all doubt!

Peanut Butter

2   cups peanuts, roasted and salted
1½ tsp. canola or peanut oil

Combine roasted peanuts and oil in a food processor fitted with a metal blade. Grind ingredients continuously for 2 to 3 minutes. The ground nuts will form a ball. As soon as the ball smooths out, the peanut butter is ready. If necessary, stop the machine and scrape down the sides with rubber spatula. Pack into a jar with a tight fitting lid. Store in the refrigerator. Makes 1½ cups.

Chunky Peanut Butter

Add ¼ cup chopped peanuts to the basic peanut butter recipe.

Honey Peanut Butter

Add 2 tablespoons honey to the food processor when making basic peanut butter. Blend briefly until mixed.

Peanut Butter Syrup

½   cup creamy peanut butter
¼   cup corn syrup*

Mix until well blended. Great on crackers.

*You can add more corn syrup to make a syrup for pancakes. Makes ¾ cup.

Apple Butter

9-10 apples, cored, peeled and chopped
2 cups sugar
2 tsp. cinnamon
⅛ tsp. cloves
⅛ tsp. salt

Place everything into a crockpot. Stir, cover and cook on high 1 hour

Then cook on low for 9-11 hours or until thick and dark brown. Stir occasionally.

Uncover and cook on low 1 hour longer.

Stir with a whisk until smooth. Refrigerate or freeze. Makes 2 pints.

Easy Orange Marmalade

1 organic orange*
1 Tbsp. water
½ cup sugar

Cut the unpeeled orange and blend in a blender or food processor with the water. Pour mixture into a saucepan with the sugar and boil for 15 minutes. Makes ½ cup.

*If a non-organic orange is used, be sure to wash it very well with some dish soap and a vegetable brush before cutting into pieces.

Peach Jam

2   cups peaches
2   cups sugar
2   Tbsp. cornstarch

Peel and slice peaches. Put into a saucepan and boil the peaches down to the pulp and juices. Add sugar and cornstarch and boil until thickened. Refrigerate or freeze. This recipe may be doubled or increased to whatever size you need. Makes 2-3 cups.

Strawberry Jam

3   qts. fresh strawberries
¾   cup sugar
1   Tbsp. lemon juice

In large microwave safe bowl, combine strawberries, sugar and lemon juice. Cover loosely and microwave on high 15 seconds. Stir mixture to dissolve sugar. Microwave on high, uncovered, for 5 minutes.

Stir mixture well and check to see if it is done by putting a little on a spoon and placing it in the freezer for 5 minutes, uncovered. Look at the preserves on the spoon. They should be thick but not hard.

For slightly thicker preserves, microwave on high for another 5 minutes. For sweeter preserves, stir in a little more sugar and then cook another minute.

Spoon preserves into jars and refrigerate or cool at room temperature. Spoon into plastic bags and freeze. Makes 7 cups.

- **When you have leftover jam or jelly, put ¾ cup of hot water in the jar and shake well. Pour into popsicle molds and freeze.**

Substitutions

Substitutions

I didn't have potatoes...
so I substituted rice,

I didn't have paprika...
so I used another spice,

I didn't have tomato sauce...
I used tomato paste,

A whole can... not half a can...
I don't believe in waste!

A friend gave me the recipe

She said you couldn't beat it!

But there must be something wrong

As I couldn't even eat it ! ! !

GFDF Substitutions

Eggs

1 egg	=	1 Tbsp. soy flour and 1 Tbsp. water

Flour

1 Tbsp. cornstarch	=	2 Tbsp. flour for thickening sauces and gravies

Sugar

1 cup granulated sugar	=	1¾ cups powdered sugar or 1 cup packed light brown sugar or ¾ cup honey
1 cup powdered or confectioner's sugar	=	½ cup plus 1 Tbsp. granulated sugar
1 cup brown sugar	=	1 cup sugar plus 2 Tbsp. molasses

GFDF Substitutions

Miscellaneous

1 pkg. active dry yeast	=	½ cake compressed yeast or 1 Tbsp. bulk yeast
1 tsp. baking powder	=	¼ tsp. cream of tartar plus ¼ tsp. baking soda
1 Tbsp. lemon juice	=	½ Tbsp. vinegar
1 cup chopped apples	=	1 cup chopped pears plus 1 Tbsp. lemon juice
1 cup dry bread crumbs	=	¾ cup cracker crumbs or 1 cup corn flake crumbs
1 cup butter	=	1 cup DF butter or ⅞ cup vegetable oil 1 cup butter flavored shortening
1 Tbsp. cornstarch	=	2 Tbsp. all purpose flour
1 cup dark corn syrup	=	¾ cup light corn syrup plus ¼ cup light molasses
1 chopped onion	=	1 Tbsp. instant minced onion
1 clove garlic	=	¼ tsp. garlic powder
1 cup tomato sauce	=	½ cup tomato paste plus ½ cup water
1 Tbsp. prepared mustard	=	1 tsp. dry mustard plus 1 Tbsp. water
1 tsp. dried herbs	=	1 Tbsp. fresh herbs
1 ounce unsweetened chocolate	=	3 Tbsp. unsweetened cocoa powder plus 1 Tbsp. shortening

Equivalents

3 teaspoons	=	1 tablespoon
4 tablespoons	=	¼ cup
16 tablespoons	=	1 cup
1 gallon	=	4 quarts
	=	8 pints
	=	16 cups
	=	128 fluid ounces
1 quart	=	2 pints
	=	4 cups
	=	32 fluid ounces
1 pint	=	2 cups
	=	16 fluid ounces
1 gill	=	½ cup
	=	4 fluid ounces
	=	8 tablespoons
1 fluid ounce	=	2 tablespoons
1 tablespoon	=	½ fluid ounce
	=	3 teaspoons

To convert **ounces** to **grams**, multiply ounces x 28.35

To convert **pounds** to **grams**, multiply pounds x 453.59

To convert **Fahrenheit degrees** to **Celsius degrees**:
$$°C = (°F-32) \times 5/9$$

1 stick butter = 8 tablespoons = **4** ounces = ¼ pound

Notes

Index

362

O

Oat Milk, 316
Oatmeal
    Apple Bars, 286
    Apple Crisp, 290
    Cookies, 277
    Granola Bars, 297
    Granola, 66
    Ideas, 64
    Meatballs, 174
    Meatloaf, 185
    Muffins, 59
    No Bake Fudge Cookies, 271
    Oat Milk, 316
    Overnight, 65
    Peanut Butter And Chocolate, 64
    Salting, 48
    Smoothies, 43
    Tips, 14, 239
    What Cake, 229
Oil, Chile Garlic, 162
Oil, Flavored, 152
Oil, Refrigerating Leftover, 118
Oil, Storage, 152
Old Fashioned Salad Dressing, 165
Onion(s)
    Baked, 124
    Barbecue Sauce, 324
    Barbecued, 124
    Bean Goulash, 183
    Bean Salad, 153
    Beans And Rice, 145
    Beans, Green, 119
    Beans, Baked, 119
    Beans, Dry, 138
    Beans, Refried, 139
    Broccoli And Pasta, 141
    Broccoli Soup, 102
    Carrot Casserole, Creamy, 121

Onion(s) (continued)
    Carrot Salad, 153
    Cheesy Cauliflower, 122
    Cheesy Rice And Tomatoes, 144
    Chicken Salad, 114
    Chili Sauce, 323
    Chili, 108
    Cucumber Salad, 154
    Cucumbers and Tomatoes, 122
    Cutting, 152
    Dijon Mustard, 329
    Dilled, 168
    Egg Rolls, 123
    Enchiladas, Beef, 206
    Enchiladas, Stacked, 205
    Fish, Baked, 213
    Freezing, 29
    French Dip, 115
    Fried, 135
    Garden Salad, 155
    Green Beans, 119
    Green Chile, 204
    Hash, 183
    Hush Puppies, 91
    Italian Chicken, 195
    Italian Sausage, 212
    Italian Vinaigrette, 163
    Liver And Onions, 187
    Macaroni Salad, 156
    Meatballs, 174
    Mexican Summer Squash, 134
    Pasta Fagioli, 142
    Pickles, 169
    Pizza Or Spaghetti Sauce, 210
    Pizza, 116, 209
    Pork Chops, 203
    Potato Salad, 157
    Potatoes, Baked, 125
    Potatoes, Scalloped, 130

U, V

Vacuum Seal Freezer Bags, 28
Vanilla Glaze, 238
Vanilla Pudding, 307
Vanilla, 318
Vegetable(s)
    Bacon Bean Soup, 107
    Baked Beans, 119
    Baked Fish And, 213
    Baked Potato Toppings, 125
    Bean Goulash, 183
    Bean Salad, 153
    Bean Sprouts, How To Make, 152
    Beans, Baked, 119
    Beans, Cooking Dry, 138
    Beans, Green, 119
    Beans, Leftover, 145
    Beans, Red And Rice, 145
    Beans, Refried, 139
    Broccoli And Pasta, 141
    Broccoli Salad, 157
    Broccoli Soup, 102
    Broccoli, Herbed, 120
    Butters, Flavored Vegetable, 121
    Carrot Casserole, Creamy, 121
    Carrot Salad, 153
    Carrots, Glazed, 120
    Cauliflower, Cheesy, 122
    Celery, Ants On A Log, 19
    Cheesy Rice And Tomatoes, 144
    Cole Slaw, 154
    Corn, Grilled, 123
    Cucumber Salad, 154
    Cucumbers And Tomatoes, 122
    Dilled Veggies, 168
    French Fries, 125
    Fried Vegetables, 135
    Garlic Salad, 156

Vegetable(s) (continued)
    Green Beans, 119
    Ham And Beans, 202
    Japanese Goulash, 146
    Liver And Onions, 187
    Macaroni Salad, 156
    Mexican Summer Squash, 134
    Onion Rings, 135
    Onion Slices, Baked, 124
    Onions, Baked, 124
    Onions, Barbecued, 124
    Onions, Fried, 135
    Pasta Fagioli, 142
    Pickles, 169
    Pizza Or Spaghetti Sauce, 210
    Pizza, Garden Vegetable, 209
    Potato Pancakes, 129
    Potato Peels, 129
    Potato Salad, 157
    Potatoes, Au Gratin, 130
    Potatoes, Baked Toppings, 125
    Potatoes, Baked, 125
    Potatoes, Cheesy, 129
    Potatoes, Fried, 126
    Potatoes, Lemon, 126
    Potatoes, Mashed, 128
    Potatoes, Oven Fried, 128
    Potatoes, Roast, 185
    Potatoes, Scalloped, 130
    Salad, Garden Vegetable, 155
    Salad, Garden, 155
    Salsa, 181, 332
    Shepherd's Pie, 186
    Soup, Bacon Bean, 107
    Soup, Broccoli, 102
    Soup, Chicken, 103
    Soup, Egg Drop, 111
    Soup, French Onion, 107

W, X, Y, Z

Notes

Notes

Notes

Notes

Notes

Notes

Notes

Notes

An Invitation For You

Most people say that coming to a relationship with God is important so that you know where you will go when you die. Really, a relationship with God is so much more than that. It is a relationship with the One who created everything, who created you and who has every desire for your good.

God created us all to be in a perfect relationship with him, but Adam and Eve broke that relationship by turning from Him and breaking that relationship. This is what the Bible calls sin. As a result of that original sin and the sins that we all continue to commit, we are separated from God and hopelessly lost. In His word, God tells us "No one is righteous— not even one" (Romans 3:10) and that a price must be paid for our sin. Unfortunately, the price for our sin is too high for us to ever pay and, without God, we are destined to pay our own price forever separated from God in what the Bible calls the lake of fire. (Revelation 20:15)

The Good News is that God sent His perfect, one and only Son, Jesus, to pay that price for us. When He died for our sins and rose from the dead, He overcame death and freed us from having to pay our own sin debt, if we are willing to accept His payment for us. It is a free gift (Romans 6:23) that we cannot earn, but that He willingly offers to us. God's desire is not to condemn you (John 3:17), but He will not force you to accept His free gift.

You don't have to be "good enough" to come to Him. God's word says that "while we were yet sinners, Christ died for us" (Romans 5:8). He invites you to come just as you are and promises to make you a new creation and give you eternal life in Heaven with Him. God's word says, "to all who believed him and accepted him, he gave the right to become children of God." (John 1:12)

So how do you accept His free gift?

1) Admit you have sinned.
2) Believe in Jesus, and that He Paid that price for you.
3) Confess that Jesus is Lord and give your life to Him.

You can pray this to Him sincerely in your own words, saying something like, "Dear Lord Jesus, I know that I am a sinner, and I ask for Your forgiveness. I believe You died for my sins and rose from the dead. I turn from my sins and invite You to come into my heart and life. I want to trust and follow You as my Lord and Savior. In Your Name. Amen."

If you do this, God's Word promises that you will be saved, your sins will be forgiven

(1 Peter 2:24), and you will spend eternity in Heaven (John 3:16) with the promise that it can never be taken away (John 10:27-28).

If you haven't given your life to Christ, won't you come to Him today?

Got questions? Please feel free to contact us: editor@livingonadime.com